Apache
Pocket Reference

Andrew Ford

O'REILLY®

Beijing • Cambridge • Farnham • Köln • Paris • Sebastopol • Taipei • Tokyo

Apache Pocket Reference

by Andrew Ford

Copyright © 2000 Ford & Mason Ltd. All rights reserved.
Printed in the United States of America.

Published by O'Reilly & Associates, Inc., 101 Morris Street,
Sebastopol, CA 95472.

Editor: Gigi Estabrook

Production Editor: Madeleine Newell

Cover Designer: Ellie Volckhausen

Printing History:

      June 2000:   First Edition.

Library of Congress Cataloging-in-Publication Data

Ford, Andrew.
    Apache pocket reference / Andrew Ford.--p. cm.
    ISBN 1-56592-706-0
    1. Apache (Computer file : Apache Group)--Handbooks,
        manuals, etc. 2. Web servers--Computer programs--
        Handbooks, manuals, etc. I. Title.

TK5105.8885.A63 F67 2000
005.7'13769--dc21   00-033975

1-56592-706-0   [8/00]
[C]

Table of Contents

Apache Pocket Reference

Apache is far and away the most widely used web server in the world, running on Windows NT as well as Unix and other platforms. Probably one of the most popular pieces of open source software in existence, it powers over half of the world's web sites and is still increasing its market share. Apache forms the basis of a number of commercial web servers, such as C2Net's Stronghold, Covalent's Raven, IBM HTTP Server powered by Apache, and Red Hat Secure Server.

Apache is at the leading edge of web server development and is often where new technologies are first implemented. It has a flexible architecture that allows independent developers to add their own functionality by way of modules, written either in C or, with the advent of *mod_perl*, in Perl.

This pocket reference summarizes Apache's command-line options and configuration directives. It covers Apache version 1.3.12, but is applicable to other versions as well as to web servers derived from Apache.

For more information on Apache, visit the Apache Software Foundation web site at *http://www.apache.org*.

Acknowledgments

I would like to thank Stas Bekman, Gigi Estabrook, Tony Finch, Martin Kraemer, Doug MacEachern, Catherine Mason, Lenny Muellner, Madeleine Newell, and all my reviewers.

Conventions

Apache directive syntax uses a number of conventions:

constant width text
> Denotes literal text

constant width italic text
> Denotes dummy parameters

{ *A* | *B* }
> Denotes alternatives

[text]
> Denotes optional text

... Indicates that the previous element may be repeated

Apache configuration directives are described in a standard format, as shown here.

DirectiveName   module_name

DirectiveName arg1 arg2 arg3 ...

Contexts: GVSF* (Override)   *Compatibility:* 1.x +
Default: default

The top line gives the name of the directive, along with the name of the Apache module that implements the directive (the module name is omitted if the directive is implemented by the core module). The next line gives the directive syntax: the name of the directive is given in bold type followed by its arguments. Directives are case-insensitive, as are most arguments except those that refer to case-sensitive objects such as filenames. Subsequent lines give the list of contexts in which the directive may be used, version compatibility notes, and the default value for the directive (if applicable).

The list of valid contexts can contain one or more of the following abbreviations:

G   Valid in global context; i.e., in the server configuration files outside of any virtual host or directory-type container

V   Valid in a virtual host section

S   Valid in a directory-type section (`<Directory>`, `<Files>`, and `<Location>`)

F   Valid in a per-directory configuration file (named *.htaccess* by default)

*   Indicates that the directive may be given more than once in a context

An override keyword is given in parentheses after the context abbreviations, if the directive can be used in a per-directory configuration file and is controlled by an AllowOverride directive category.

Starting and Stopping Apache

Apache is usually set up to be started automatically when the system is booted, and stopped when the system is halted. On Unix systems this is normally handled by an *rc-file*. A shell script, apachectl, is provided with Apache to automate the process.

Should you need to start Apache manually, it takes the following command-line options:

-c*directive*
    Process *directive* after reading configuration files.

-C*directive*
    Process *directive* before reading configuration files.

-d*directory*
    Initial value for ServerRoot.

-D*parameter*
    Define parameter for `<IfDefine>` sections.

-f*file*
> Configuration file (default is *conf/httpd.conf*).

-k {shutdown | restart}
> Windows only; shutdown or restart Apache (1.3.3 +).

-l   List compiled-in modules and exit.

-L   List available configuration directives (provided by compiled-in modules) and exit.

-n*name*
> Windows only; service name for Apache (1.3.7 +).

-S   Show virtual host settings and exit.

-t   Test syntax of configuration files, checking for the existence of document root directories, and exit.

-T   Test the syntax of configuration files, but without checking for the existence of document root directories, and exit.

-v   Print version and build date, and exit.

-V   Show compilation settings and exit.

-X   Run in single-process debug mode.

On Unix systems, Apache responds to the following signals sent to the parent process (the process ID of which is stored in the *pid* file):

TERM
> Stops the server by causing the parent process to attempt to kill each of the child processes and then terminate.

HUP Restarts the server by causing the parent process to kill off each of the child processes and then reread the configuration files and spawn new child processes. Server statistics are reset to zero on a restart.

USR1
> Initiates a graceful restart. Child processes are advised to terminate after processing the current request, or immediately if not currently servicing a request. The parent

---

process rereads the configuration files and starts to spawn new child processes to maintain the appropriate number of server processes. Server statistics are not reset on a graceful restart.

On Windows NT, use the -k command-line option, or if Apache is installed as a service, use the NET START and NET STOP commands.

Apache Modules

Apache modules may have differing statuses (which may change between releases):

BASE
> Base modules are included in the Apache distribution and are compiled in by default.

OPTIONAL
> Optional modules are included in the Apache distribution but are not compiled in by default.

EXPERIMENTAL
> Experimental modules are included in the Apache distribution but are not compiled in by default.

Roughly three dozen modules are included in the Apache distribution, as follows.

Module Name	Status	Description
mod_access	BASE	Access control based on client hostname or IP address
mod_actions	BASE	Executes scripts based on MIME type or request method
mod_alias	BASE	URL mapping
mod_asis	BASE	Canned responses from files that include HTTP headers
mod_auth	BASE	User authentication using text-based configuration files

Module Name	Status	Description
mod_auth_anon	OPTIONAL	Anonymous authentication
mod_auth_db	OPTIONAL	User authentication using Berkeley DB files
mod_auth_dbm	OPTIONAL	User authentication using DBM files
mod_auth_digest	EXPERIMENTAL	MD5 authentication
mod_autoindex	BASE	Automatic directory listings
mod_cern_meta	OPTIONAL	Support for HTTP header metafiles
mod_cgi	BASE	Executes CGI scripts
mod_digest	OPTIONAL	MD5 authentication
mod_dir	BASE	Basic directory handling
mod_env	BASE	Passing of environments to CGI scripts
mod_expires	OPTIONAL	Applies Expires headers to resources
mod_headers	OPTIONAL	Adds arbitrary HTTP headers to resources
mod_imap	BASE	Imagemap file handler
mod_include	BASE	Server-side include documents
mod_info	OPTIONAL	Server configuration information
mod_isapi	OPTIONAL	Windows ISAPI Extension support
mod_log_agent	OPTIONAL	Logging of the client user agent (deprecated—use *mod_log_config* instead)
mod_log_config	BASE	User-configurable logging
mod_log_referer	OPTIONAL	Logging of the HTTP referer field (deprecated—use *mod_log_config* instead)
mod_mime	BASE	Determines document types using file extensions

Module Name	Status	Description
mod_mime_magic	OPTIONAL	Determines document types in the manner of the Unix `file` command
mod_mmap_static	EXPERIMENTAL	Maps files into memory for faster delivery
mod_negotiation	BASE	Content negotiation
mod_proxy	OPTIONAL	Caching proxy
mod_rewrite	OPTIONAL	Powerful URI-to-filename mapping using regular expressions
mod_setenvif	BASE	Sets environment variables based on client information
mod_so	OPTIONAL	Support for loading modules at runtime
mod_speling	OPTIONAL	Automatically corrects minor mistakes in URLs
mod_status	OPTIONAL	Server status display
mod_unique_id	OPTIONAL	Generates a unique identifier for every request
mod_userdir	BASE	User home directories
mod_usertrack	OPTIONAL	User tracking using cookies
mod_vhost_alias	OPTIONAL	Dynamically configured mass virtual hosting

Further modules can be found on the Apache Module Registry (*http://modules.apache.org*).

Directory Layout

Conventions for Apache directory structuring vary between releases and distributions. The source distribution will install in the following subdirectories under */usr/local/apache*, unless configured differently.

Directory	Contents
bin	Program files
sbin	Administrative program files (often placed in the *bin* subdirectory)
libexec	Loadable modules
man	Manual pages (often stored in the system *man* directories)
conf	Configuration files (often stored in the */etc* directory hierarchy)
icons	Icon image files
htdocs	HTML documents
cgi-bin	CGI scripts
include	Apache C language include files (needed for compiling third-party modules)
run	Runtime status files (often stored with the log files)
logs	Log files
proxy	Proxy cache hierarchy (if caching is enabled)

Support Utilities

The Apache distribution includes a number of support utilities that are usually installed in the *bin* or *sbin* subdirectory. These are shown in the following table.

Program	Description
ab	Simple benchmarking tool
apachectl	Apache runtime control script
apxs	Apache Extension Tool—used to build Dynamic Shared Objects (DSOs)
dbmmanage	Utility to manage DBM-format user-authentication files
htdigest	Utility to manage flat-file user-authentication files for digest authentication

Program	Description
htpasswd	Utility to manage flat-file user-authentication files for basic authentication
logresolve	Batch utility to post-process access log files to resolve IP addresses
logresolve.pl	Perl script to post-process access log files to resolve IP addresses
rotatelogs	Logging filter to rotate log files
split-logfile	Simple Perl script to split a combined log file for multiple virtual hosts where the first field is the hostname
suexec	Wrapper program to execute CGI scripts under a different user and group to those under which the server processes run (invoked directly from Apache)

General Configuration

Configuration File Directives

When Apache starts or restarts, it reads the main server configuration file from the default location, or from the location specified with the -f command-line argument. Comments can be included in configuration files by starting the line with a hash sign (#). Blank lines and leading white space are ignored.

The following directives affect the location of secondary configuration files.

ServerRoot

ServerRoot *directory*

Contexts: G
Default: /usr/local/apache

Root directory for the server. Relative paths for other directives, such as AccessConfig, are taken relative to this directory. May be overridden with the -d command-line option.

AccessConfig

AccessConfig `filename`

Contexts: GV
Default: `conf/access.conf`

Secondary configuration file that historically contained access control–related directives. It can now contain any directive valid in the main configuration file. Specify `filename` as */dev/null* (or as *nul* on Windows) to disable.

ResourceConfig

ResourceConfig `filename`

Contexts: GV
Default: `conf/srm.conf`

Secondary configuration file that historically contained most directives. It can now contain any directive valid in the main configuration file. Specify `filename` as */dev/null* (or as *nul* on Windows) to disable.

Include

Include `filename`

Contexts: GVS*   *Compatibility:* 1.3 +

Reads and processes the contents of the named configuration file, which is logically included in place of the directive.

AccessFileName

AccessFileName `filename`

Contexts: GV*
Default: `.htaccess`

Names the per-directory configuration file. Although the directive name and default value imply otherwise, the file is not restricted to access control directives. Note that prior to Apache 1.3 only a single filename was allowed.

AllowOverride

`AllowOverride` *directive-category*

Contexts: S
Default: All

Specifies whether the per-directory configuration file is read for particular directories and if read, specifies which of the following categories
of directives are allowed in per-directory configuration files in directories matched by the enclosing sectional directive. If the per-directory
configuration file contains directives that are not allowed, an internal
server error is generated.

Category	Meaning
All	All directives valid in per-directory configuration files
AuthConfig	Authentication and authorization directives
FileInfo	Directives controlling document attributes
Indexes	Directory indexing directives
Limit	Access control directives
Options	Directory features

If this directive is set to None, the per-directory configuration file in
directories matched by the current section is ignored. Note that the
`AllowOverride` directive is ignored in <Files> sections.

Conditional sections

Conditional sections enclose directives that Apache may
ignore while parsing the configuration files if the condition
specified on the section is not met. Conditional sections may
be nested.

<IfDefine

```
<IfDefine [!]parameter>
 . . .
</IfDefine>
```

Contexts: GVSF   *Compatibility:* 1.3.1 +

Enclosed directives are evaluated only if the named parameter was defined with the -D command-line option, or was not defined but *parameter* is preceded by an exclamation point (!).

<IfModule

```
<IfModule [!]module>
  . . .
</IfModule>
```

Contexts: GVSF   *Compatibility:* 1.2 +

Enclosed directives are evaluated only if the named module is active, or is inactive but *module* is preceded by an exclamation point (!). Note that the name includes the trailing .c as printed by the -l command-line option and as used in AddModule.

Main Server, Virtual Hosts, and Containers

In order to respond to requests, Apache must listen to a network port. Apache can listen on multiple IP addresses and ports and can be configured to respond differently according to the IP address and port the client connected to.

A single IP address may be represented by many different hostnames. In this case, the hostname requested can be determined only by examining the Host HTTP header, which is new for HTTP 1.1. Note that name-based virtual hosts do not work with SSL/TLS connections, as the hostname is needed to set up the secure connection but can only be extracted from the headers once the key exchange has occurred.

Ports and IP addresses

The following directives tell Apache on which IP addresses and ports it should listen.

BindAddress

```
BindAddress{ *|IP-addr|fqdn }
```

Contexts: G
Default: *

The network address on which the server listens for connections. If the value is specified as an asterisk (*), it will listen on all addresses of all network interfaces.

Listen

`Listen [IP-addr:] port-number`

Contexts: G*   *Compatibility:* 1.1 +

Specifies the network port and address on which the server listens for connections.

Port

`Port portno`

Contexts: GV
Default: 80

Specifies the port number used in self-referential URLs and as the value of the SERVER_PORT CGI variable. In the absence of any BindAddress or Listen directives in the main server, it also sets the port on which the server listens.

Virtual hosts

Virtual hosts are configured with the <VirtualHost> sections, but these have an effect only if Apache is listening on the IP address and port specified.

<VirtualHost

```
<VirtualHost addr[:port]...>
 ...
</VirtualHost>
```

Contexts: G   *Compatibility:* 1.1 +

Contains directives that only apply to a particular virtual host. *addr* may be an IP address or the fully qualified domain name for the virtual host; it may also be the literal _default_, which will match any IP address not explicitly listed in another virtual host section. A port number can be specified with :*port*.

NameVirtualHost

NameVirtualHost *addr[:port]*

Contexts: G   *Compatibility:* 1.3 +

Sets the IP address for subsequent name-based virtual host sections.

ServerAlias

ServerAlias *fqdn...*

Contexts: V   *Compatibility:* 1.1 +

Sets alternative names for a host used with name-based virtual hosts.

ServerName

ServerName *name*

Contexts: GV
Default: determined automatically by DNS lookup

Specifies the hostname to use when creating redirection URLs. See also UseCanonicalName.

ServerPath

ServerPath *pathname*

Contexts: V   *Compatibility:* 1.1 +

Sets the URL path for older browsers that do not send a Host header. Requests that start with this path will use the current virtual host.

UseCanonicalName

UseCanonicalName { ON|OFF|DNS }

Contexts: GVS   *Compatibility:* 1.3 +
Default: ON

If this is set to ON, Apache uses the server name and port specified with the ServerName and Port directives when constructing self-referential URLs. If it is set to OFF, Apache uses the server name specified in the Host header (if specified) and the port on which the connection was made. If it is set to DNS, Apache performs a reverse DNS lookup on the IP address to which the connection was made to

---

determine the server name, and uses the port on which the connection was made.

Mass virtual hosting

The *mod_vhost_alias* module allows the document root and CGI script directories for all matching virtual hosts to be specified as patterns into which parts of the hostname or IP address are interpolated, as indicated by these %-specifiers.

Spec.	Description
%p	Replaced with the port number of the virtual host.
%n	Replaced with the *n*th component of the hostname or IP address. If *n* is zero, the whole string is used. If *n* is preceded by a minus sign, it counts from the end of the hostname or IP address. If the specifier is suffixed by a plus sign, the rest of the hostname or IP address is used.
%n.m	Replaced with the *m*th character of what would be selected by %n. *m* may be prefixed by a minus sign and suffixed by a plus sign, as above.
%%	Replaced with a single percent sign (%).

mod_vhost_alias includes the following directives.

VirtualDocumentRoot   mod_vhost_alias

`VirtualDocumentRoot` *directory-pattern*

Contexts: GV   *Compatibility:* 1.3.9 +

URLs for a matching virtual host are translated to filenames by prepending a document root directory formed by interpolating the value of the server name into *directory-pattern*.

VirtualDocumentRootIP   mod_vhost_alias

`VirtualDocumentRootIP` *directory-pattern*

Contexts: GV   *Compatibility:* 1.3.9 +

Identical to `VirtualDocumentRoot`, except the IP address is used rather than the server name.

VirtualScriptAlias

mod_vhost_alias

VirtualScriptAlias *directory-pattern*

Contexts: GV   *Compatibility:* 1.3.9 +

URLs for a matching virtual host that start with */cgi-bin/* are translated to filenames by prepending a script directory formed by interpolating the value of the server name into *directory-pattern*. The handler is marked as cgi-script so that the file will be processed as such.

VirtualScriptAliasIP

mod_vhost_alias

VirtualScriptAliasIP *directory-pattern*

Contexts: GV   *Compatibility:* 1.3.9 +

Identical to VirtualScriptAlias, except the IP address is used rather than the server name.

Container sections

Container sections allow the scope of directives to be limited by directory, filename, location, or request method. When processing a request, the directives are applied in the following sequence:

1. Non-regular-expression <Directory> sections and per-directory configuration files, working from shortest to longest pathname. The per-directory configuration files override the sections.

2. Regular-expression <Directory> sections.

3. <Files> and <FilesMatch> sections.

4. <Location> and <LocationMatch> sections.

<Directory

<Directory { *pattern*|~ *regex* } >
...
</Directory>

Contexts: GV

Container for directives that apply only to matching directories (and subdirectories). Directories can be matched against a filename pattern or a regular expression.

<DirectoryMatch

```
<DirectoryMatch regex>
 . . .
</DirectoryMatch>
```

Contexts: GV   *Compatibility:* 1.3 +

Enclosed directives apply only to directories (and their subdirectories) that match the specified regular expression.

<Files

```
<Files { pattern|~ regex } >
 . . .
</Files>
```

Contexts: GVSF   *Compatibility:* 1.2 +

Enclosed directives apply only to files that match the specified filename pattern or regular expression.

<FilesMatch

```
<FilesMatch regex>
 . . .
</FilesMatch>
```

Contexts: GVSF   *Compatibility:* 1.3 +

Enclosed directives apply only to matching files.

<Location

```
<Location { pattern|~ regex } >
 . . .
</Location>
```

Contexts: GV   *Compatibility:* 1.1 +

Enclosed directives apply only to URLs that match the specified pattern or regular expression.

<LocationMatch

```
<LocationMatch regex>
 . . .
</LocationMatch>
```

Contexts: GV   *Compatibility:* 1.3 +

Enclosed directives apply only to matching URLs.

<Limit

```
<Limit method...>
 . . .
</Limit>
```

Contexts: GVSF

Enclosed directives apply only to matching methods.

<LimitExcept

```
<LimitExcept method...>
 . . .
</LimitExcept>
```

Contexts: GVSF   *Compatibility:* 1.3.5 +

Enclosed directives apply for non-matching methods.

Options

```
Options [+|-]feature...
```

Contexts: GVSF (Options)
Default: All

Controls the advanced features that are enabled in a particular context. The options defined in the most restricted context are taken in their entirety unless all features are prefixed with a plus or minus symbol, in which case those features prefixed with a plus are enabled, those with a minus are disabled, and the remaining features are inherited from the next context out. The options are:

None
: No extra features are enabled.

All Enables all options except MultiViews.

ExecCGI
: Permits execution of CGI scripts.

FollowSymLinks
: Controls whether Apache will follow symbolic links (ignored within a <Location> section).

Includes
: Permits server-side includes.

IncludesNOEXEC
: Controls the server-side includes #exec command and the use of #include with filenames that refer to CGI scripts.

Indexes
: Controls whether directory listings are generated for URLs that map to directories where there is no directory index file.

MultiViews
: Enables content-negotiated MultiViews.

SymLinksIfOwnerMatch
: Follow symbolic links only if the owner of the target matches the owner of the link (ignored within a <Location> section).

General Configuration Directives

User and Group

The User and Group directives set the user and group under which Apache processes requests. Resources to be served by Apache must be readable by this user and group, but for security reasons, system resources (such as the system password) should not be readable, and certainly not writable, by the user or group.

If used in a virtual host section with the *suEXEC* wrapper installed and properly configured, Apache will switch to this user and group when running CGI scripts.

User

```
User  { username|#userid }
```

Contexts: GV
Default: #-1

Username or user ID to which Apache changes while processing requests.

Group

```
Group  { group-name|#group-id }
```

Contexts: GV
Default: #-1

Group name or group ID to which Apache changes while processing requests.

Error logging

As well as logging individual requests, Apache logs significant events to an error log. These directives specify the error log and the level of logging.

ErrorLog

```
ErrorLog  { filename|syslog[:facility] }
```

Contexts: GV
Default: logs/error_log

Log file for error messages. If *filename* starts with a pipe character (|), it is taken as an executable file that is spawned and passed error messages on its standard input.

LogLevel

```
LogLevel  level
```

Contexts: GV   *Compatibility:* 1.3 +
Default: error

Controls the level of logging to the error log. Only messages that are of a severity of *level* or higher will be logged. The log levels are listed in the following table in descending order of severity.

Level	Description
emerg	Emergency conditions signifying the system is unusable
alert	Conditions that signify immediate action is required
crit	Critical conditions
error	Error conditions
warn	Warnings
notice	Normal but significant conditions
info	Informational messages
debug	Debug messages

Administrative files

Depending on the operating system, Apache uses a number of files, specified by the following directives, for communication between server processes and also with utility programs. To reduce security risks, these files should not be located in directories that are world-writable or writable by the user or group specified with the User and Group directives.

LockFile

LockFile *filename*

Contexts: G
Default: logs/accept.lock

Lock file used for serializing access to incoming requests, The process ID of the parent process is appended to the name. The path should be changed if the default location is not on a local disk.

PidFile

PidFile *filename*

Contexts: G
Default: logs/httpd.pid

File in which the process ID of the main server process is recorded. The apachectl utility relies on the *pid* file being in the standard location.

ScoreBoardFile

ScoreBoardFile *filename*

Contexts: G
Default: logs/apache_status

File used for communicating status information between the parent and child server processes. Only used on systems that do not support shared memory.

CoreDumpDirectory

CoreDumpDirectory *directory*

Contexts: G   *Compatibility:* 1.3 +
Default: ServerRoot

Directory in which Apache will dump core in case of a fatal error. The default directory should not be writable by the user specified with the User directive, so no core file will normally be written. Note that core dumps of SSL servers may contain private keys, which may be a security concern.

Server information

ServerAdmin

ServerAdmin *email-addr*

Contexts: GV

Sets the email address included in error messages generated by Apache.

ServerSignature

ServerSignature { ON|OFF|Email }

Contexts: GVSF   *Compatibility:* 1.3 +
Default: OFF

Controls the generation of a footer line containing the server address on server-generated documents such as error responses and generated directory listings. If this is set to Email, the email address set with the ServerAdmin directive is included as a mailto: link.

ServerTokens

```
ServerTokens  { Min[imal]|OS|Full }
```

Contexts: G   *Compatibility:* 1.3 +
Default: Full

Controls the amount of information about the server returned with
response headers. Minimal sends the server name and version, OS
adds the operating system type, and Full adds information from compiled-in modules.

HostnameLookups

```
HostnameLookups  { ON|OFF|Double }
```

Contexts: GVS
Default: OFF

Controls whether DNS lookups are performed to resolve hostnames
for logging and passing to CGI and SSI scripts. If this directive is set
to Double, following a successful reverse DNS lookup, a forward
lookup is performed to check that the IP address matches the hostname. Regardless of the setting, a double DNS lookup will always be
used for access control by hostname. Note that prior to 1.3, the
default was ON and the value Double was not available.

IdentityCheck

```
IdentityCheck  { ON|OFF }
```

Contexts: GVS
Default: OFF

Enables logging of the remote username. If this directive is enabled,
Apache attempts to retrieve the information from the client machine.
Retrieving the information causes delays, and the information is often
unavailable or unreliable, so except when serving an intranet, this feature is best left disabled.

Module management

Modules may be compiled into Apache or may be compiled
separately as Dynamic Shared Objects (DSOs), which are normally shared object files on Unix and DLL files on Windows.

LoadModule   mod_so

LoadModule *module filename*

Contexts: G*   *Compatibility:* 1.3 +

Loads the named DSO module by linking in the object file or library
and adding the module structure to the list of active modules.

LoadFile   mod_so

LoadFile *filename*...

Contexts: G*   *Compatibility:* 1.3 +

Links in the named object or library files, which may contain code
required by modules.

ClearModuleList

ClearModuleList

Contexts: G   *Compatibility:* 1.2 +

Clears the internal list of active modules.

AddModule

AddModule *module*...

Contexts: G*   *Compatibility:* 1.2 +

Activates the specified modules.

Performance Tuning Directives

Network performance

Apache listens on a network port for requests and transmits its
response over the network connection. There are a limited
number of parameters that can be changed to optimize the
performance of the network connection.

ListenBacklog

ListenBacklog *number*

Contexts: G   *Compatibility:* 1.2.1 +
Default: 511

Sets the maximum number of entries for the operating system's *listen* queue of pending connections. If connection requests arrive faster than Apache can process them, the queue will overflow. Further requests will be rejected by the operating system until there is space in the queue.

SendBufferSize

SendBufferSize *bytes*

Contexts: G
Default: determined by operating system

Sets the size of TCP buffers.

ServerType

ServerType { inetd|standalone }

Contexts: G
Default: standalone

Indicates whether Apache is run as a daemon or as a single-shot process spawned by the inetd daemon. Note that running from inetd is no longer fully supported.

Timeout

Timeout *secs*

Contexts: G
Default: 300 seconds, i.e., five minutes

Sets a timeout used in three instances: for receiving a request once a connection is accepted; between receipt of packets in the case of POST or PUT requests; and between acknowledgment packets when sending the response.

Persistent connections

Persistent connections allow a network connection to be re-used for subsequent requests by the same client, thus avoiding the overhead of establishing separate connections.

KeepAlive

```
KeepAlive  { ON|OFF }
```

Contexts: GV   *Compatibility:* 1.1 +
Default: ON

Enables persistent connections. Note that prior to version 1.2, the argument was the maximum number of requests to be processed on a persistent connection or zero to disable persistent connections.

KeepAliveTimeout

```
KeepAliveTimeout  seconds
```

Contexts: GV   *Compatibility:* 1.1 +
Default: 15

Sets the timeout for subsequent requests on a persistent connection.

MaxKeepAliveRequests

```
MaxKeepAliveRequests  number
```

Contexts: G   *Compatibility:* 1.2 +
Default: 100

Sets the maximum number of requests that are processed on a persistent connection. A value of zero is taken to mean no limit.

Process management

On Unix systems, Apache maintains a pool of server processes to service requests. The parent process does not handle requests itself, but monitors the child processes and attempts to ensure that there are always a number of idle processes ready to handle incoming requests. If the number of idle processes drops too low, the parent process spawns new processes, as long as the number of processes does not exceed the compile-time constant HARD_SERVER_LIMIT, which defines the size of fixed-sized process tables. If there are too many idle processes, some of them are signalled to terminate. When there are no idle servers to accept incoming requests, the requests are queued by the operating system on the listen queue.

On Windows NT, there are only two processes. The first process simply monitors the second, while the second process contains a number of threads that process requests.

MaxClients

MaxClients *number*

Contexts: G
Default: 256

Sets the maximum number of child server processes that may be started and thus the maximum number of requests that can be processed simultaneously.

MaxRequestsPerChild

MaxRequestsPerChild *number*

Contexts: G
Default: 0

Sets the maximum number of connections that are processed by a child server process before it terminates voluntarily. A value of zero is interpreted as unlimited. Child processes may also terminate if the load drops; however, setting this parameter can ameliorate the effect of memory leaks in servers, especially if *mod_perl* or other resource-hungry modules are used.

MaxSpareServers

MaxSpareServers *number*

Contexts: G
Default: 10

Sets the maximum number of idle child server processes that may exist. If the server load drops, the parent process will signal excess idle processes to terminate.

MinSpareServers

MinSpareServers *number*

Contexts: G
Default: 5

Minimum number of idle child server processes that should be present. If the number drops below this level, the parent process will create new child processes to maintain a pool of processes ready to accept new connections.

StartServers

StartServers *number*

Contexts: G
Default: 5

Sets the number of child server processes created initially on startup.

ThreadsPerChild

ThreadsPerChild *number*

Contexts: G   *Compatibility:* 1.3 + (threaded servers only)
Default: 50

Sets the number of threads started by threaded versions of Apache (such as on Windows NT), and hence the maximum number of connections that can be simultaneously processed.

Request limits

Request limits, controlled by the following directives, are a defense against denial-of-service attacks. If a request exceeds any of the limits, the server returns an error response rather than attempting to service the request.

LimitRequestbody

LimitRequestbody *nbytes*

Contexts: GVSF   *Compatibility:* 1.3.2 +
Default: 0

Sets the maximum length of request body that will be accepted. A value of zero means there is no limit.

LimitRequestFields

```
LimitRequestFields number
```

Contexts: G   *Compatibility:* 1.3.2 +
Default: 100

Limits the number of request header fields that will be accepted.

LimitRequestFieldSize

```
LimitRequestFieldSize nbytes
```

Contexts: G   *Compatibility:* 1.3.2 +
Default: 8,190

Limits the length of individual request header fields that will be accepted.

LimitRequestLine

```
LimitRequestLine nbytes
```

Contexts: G   *Compatibility:* 1.3.2 +
Default: 8,190

Sets the maximum length of the request line that will be accepted.

Process resource limits

These apply to processes forked by the child server processes, not to the server processes themselves, or to processes, such as piped logs, forked by the parent server.

RLimitCPU

```
RLimitCPU { secs|max } [ secs|max ]
```

Contexts: GVSF   *Compatibility:* 1.2 +
Default: operating system defaults

Specifies soft and hard CPU resource limits, expressed in seconds per process, for processes forked by Apache (including CGI programs).

RLimitMEM

RLimitMEM { bytes|max } [bytes|max]

Contexts: GVSF   *Compatibility:* 1.2 +
Default: operating system defaults

Specifies soft and hard memory resource limits, expressed in bytes per process, for processes forked by Apache.

RLimitNPROC

RLimitNPROC { nprocs|max } [nprocs|max]

Contexts: GVSF   *Compatibility:* 1.2 +
Default: operating system defaults

Specifies soft and hard per-user process limits for processes forked by Apache. Note that if CGI processes run under the same user ID as that used by Apache for processing requests, this limit will affect Apache itself.

Request Processing

Apache processes requests in a number of phases, calling each handler registered for a particular phase in turn until all handlers have been called, or until a handler indicates either that processing of the phase is complete or that an error has occurred. The phases are listed here in order of occurrence:

Post-read
    Initial phase after the request headers have been parsed.

URL translation
    Translates the URL into the filesystem namespace.

Header parsing
    First phase in which <Directory> sections can be used (this phase is not used by any of the standard modules).

Access control
    Applies access controls not based on user credentials.

Authentication
> Checks the user's credentials.

Authorization
> Checks whether the authenticated user is allowed to access the resource.

MIME type checking
> Determines attributes of the resource, such as document content type.

Fix-up
> Makes any adjustments before the content generation phase.

Content generation
> Generates the response.

Request logging
> Logs the request.

This picture is complicated slightly in that modules can issue subrequests to return a document other than that requested or to check what the response would be if a request was made for a different resource.

Modules register handlers for the phases during which they need to influence the handling of the request. Generally a module will only register handlers for one or two phases. Directives implemented by a module are described in the chapter that covers the main phase handled by that module.

Post-Read Request Phase

This is the first phase in the request handling process. At this point, only the values of the request line and of the HTTP request headers are available. The proxy module uses this phase to prepend the string proxy: to the URI for requests it handles, so that other modules do not inadvertently handle those requests.

This phase is also used to set environment variables based on request header values. Three special environment variables can be set to modify the server's response to buggy clients:

`nokeepalive`
Disables keepalive.

`force-response-1.0`
Forces Apache to respond with an HTTP/1.0 response.

`downgrade-1.0`
Forces the request to be treated as an HTTP/1.0 request, even if the request indicates a later version.

The environment variable `UNIQUE_ID` is set to a globally unique identifier if *mod_unique_id* is compiled in.

SetEnvIf   mod_setenvif

`SetEnvIf` *attribute regex var[=value]*...

Contexts: GV   *Compatibility:* 1.3 +

Sets an environment variable if the value of the attribute matches the regular expression. The attribute may be a request header field, an environment variable set with an earlier `SetEnvIf`-type directive, or one of the following attributes of the request:

`Remote_Host`
The hostname address of the client (if available).

`Remote_Addr`
The IP address of the client.

`Remote_User`
The authenticated username (if available).

`Request_Method`
The name of the HTTP method used for the request.

`Request_Protocol`
The name and version of the protocol used for the request.

`Request_URI`
The portion of the URL that follows the scheme and host components.

If the variable name is preceded by an exclamation point (!), the variable will be unset. Otherwise, it is set to the value specified, or to 1 if no value is specified.

SetEnvIfNoCase mod_setenvif

```
SetEnvIfNoCase attribute regex var[=value]...
```

Contexts: GV   *Compatibility:* 1.3 +

Identical to the SetEnvIf directive, except that pattern matching is performed case-insensitively.

BrowserMatch mod_setenvif

```
BrowserMatch regexp var[=value]...
```

Contexts: GV*   *Compatibility:* 1.2 +

Special case of the SetEnvIf directive; the attribute tested is the User-Agent HTTP request header.

BrowserMatchNoCase mod_setenvif

```
BrowserMatchNoCase regexp var[-value]...
```

Contexts: GV*   *Compatibility:* 1.2 +

Identical to the BrowserMatch directive, except that pattern matching is performed case-insensitively.

URL Translation Phase

URL translation, the first major stage in request handling, is controlled by the following directives. Later stages, such as access controls and content type determination, use the translated URL.

DocumentRoot

```
DocumentRoot directory
```

Contexts: GV
Default: /usr/local/apache/htdocs

Top-level directory for web documents. Requests for documents not mapped by other directives are found by appending the path to this directory.

Alias   mod_alias

Alias *url-path-prefix real-path-prefix*

Contexts: GV*

Specifies a mapping from URLs to filenames. If, after URL-decoding, the document's URL matches the URL prefix, the prefix is removed and replaced with the filename path prefix.

AliasMatch   mod_alias

AliasMatch *url-regex path-replacement*

Contexts: GV*

Specifies a mapping from URLs to filenames, using regular expressions. Substrings matched by parenthesized subexpressions can be interpolated into *path-replacement* by specifying the number of the subexpression prefixed by a dollar sign ($).

CheckSpelling   mod_speling

CheckSpelling { ON|OFF }

Contexts: GVSF (Options)

Enables URLs that translate to nonexistent files to match existing files in which the filenames differ in capitalization and may contain a single insertion, deletion, transposition, or wrong character. If only one file fits the criteria, it is returned. If more than one candidate exists, a list of matches is returned, from which the client can choose.

Redirect   mod_alias

Redirect [*status*] *url-path-prefix new-prefix*

Contexts: GVSF (FileInfo)

Maps a URL to a new one, returning a redirection response to the client. *status* may be one of the following values:

---

permanent

> Returns a permanent redirect status (301), indicating that the resource has been moved permanently.

temp

> Returns a temporary redirect status (302).

seeother

> Returns a "See Other" status (303), indicating that the resource has been replaced.

gone

> Returns a "Gone" status (410), indicating that the resource has been permanently removed (the *new-url* argument should be omitted).

If *status* is not specified, a temporary redirection response is generated. The *status* argument is not available prior to Apache 1.2.

RedirectMatch   mod_alias

RedirectMatch [*status*] *url-regex new-url*

Contexts: GVSF (FileInfo)   *Compatibility:* 1.3 +

Maps a URL to a new one, using regular expressions. Substrings matched by parenthesized subexpressions can be interpolated into *new-url* by specifying the number of the subexpression prefixed by a dollar sign ($).

RedirectPermanent   mod_alias

RedirectPermanent *url-path new-url*

Contexts: GVSF (FileInfo)

Generates a permanent (status 301) redirection.

RedirectTemp   mod_alias

RedirectTemp *url-path new-url*

Contexts: GVSF (FileInfo)

Generates a temporary (status 302) redirection.

ScriptAlias   mod_alias

ScriptAlias *url-path-prefix script-dir*

Contexts: GV

Maps the *url-path* to *script-dir* and marks the handler as cgi-
script, causing matching URLs to be treated as requests for CGI
scripts.

ScriptAliasMatch   mod_alias

ScriptAliasMatch *url-regex script-dir*

Contexts: GV

Specifies a mapping from URLs to CGI scripts, using regular expressions. Substrings matched by parenthesized subexpressions can be
interpolated into *script-dir* by specifying the number of the subexpression prefixed by a dollar sign ($).

UserDir   mod_userdir

UserDir { *directory*|DISABLED [*user*]...|ENABLED *user*... }

Contexts: GV*
Default: public_html

Specifies how requests for user-specific documents (with URL paths
starting ~*username*) are handled. This directive performs many functions, depending on the value of its arguments:

Keyword DISABLED *without any usernames*
   Usernames to directory translation are disabled except for those
   explicitly enabled.

Keyword DISABLED *followed by a list of usernames*
   Usernames listed are not translated, even if they appear in a
   UserDir ENABLED directive.

Keyword ENABLED *followed by a list of usernames*
   Usernames listed will be translated unless they are explicitly
   disabled.

Relative directory name
> URL path after `~username` will be mapped to that subdirectory of the user's home directory.

Absolute pathname or URL containing an asterisk (`*`)
> The asterisk will be replaced with the username, and the part of the URL after `~username` will be appended to the path.

The URL Rewriting Engine

The *mod_rewrite* module is a sophisticated pattern-based URL rewriting engine that lets you set up complex rewriting rules specifying qualifying conditions, using the `RewriteRule` and `RewriteCond` directives. These directives allow submatches, CGI variables, and other information to be interpolated into replacement strings and condition strings, as shown in the following table.

Construct	Expansion
`$n`	Back-reference to the the *n*th parenthesized group of the `RewriteRule` pattern.
`%n`	Back-reference to the the *n*th parenthesized group part of the last matching `RewriteCond` pattern.
`%{var}`	The value of the named CGI variable.
`%{ENV:var}`	The value of the named environment variable.
`%{HTTP:header}`	The value of the named HTTP header.
`%{LA-F:var}`	*Look-ahead*: Issues an internal subrequest based on the filename to determine the final value of the named variable.
`%{LA-U:var}`	*Look-ahead*: Issues an internal subrequest based on the URL to determine the final value of the named variable.
`${map:key [ |def] }`	The value returned by the named map function (valid only in `RewriteRule`). *key* is the value to look up, which will normally be an interpolated value. *def* is the value to use if the lookup is unsuccessful.

RewriteRule mod_rewrite

`RewriteRule [!]pattern replacement[[flags]]`

Contexts: GVSF (FileInfo)

Compares the current URL with the regular expression *pattern* and substitutes *replacement*, interpolating any marked constructs, if the pattern matches (or does not match if preceded by "!") and any preceding conditions are met. A comma-separated list of flags, specified in full or abbreviated, may be enclosed in square brackets. Flags are described in the following table.

Flag	Description
{redirect | R}[=*code*]	Force a redirect.
{forbidden | F}	Terminates with 403 (FORBIDDEN) status.
{gone | G}	Returns 401 (GONE) status.
{proxy | P}	Pass off to *mod_proxy*.
{last | L}	Finish applying rewriting rules.
{next | N}	Start applying rules from the top against the current URL.
{chain | C}	Chain current rule with the next rule.
{type | T}=*type*	Set the MIME type to *type*.
{nosubreq | NS}	Skip the rule if processing an internal sub-request.
{nocase | NC}	Match case-insensitively.
{qsappend | QSA}	Append to existing query string.
{passthrough | PT}	Pass the result through to the next handler.
{skip | S}=*n*	Skip *n* rules.
{env | E}=*var*:*val*	Set environment variable.

The replacement may be specified as "-", in which case no substitution is performed, but any chained rules are evaluated.

RewriteCond mod_rewrite

`RewriteCond string[!]condition[[flags]]`

Contexts: GVSF (FileInfo)

Specifies a condition for the following `RewriteRule` to match. The only flags are `nocase` (or NC) to compare strings case-insensitively, and `ornext` (or OR) to combine the current condition with the next one using a logical OR (by default, conditions are ANDed together). *string* may contain interpolated sequences. *condition* may be a regular expression or one of the following:

-d *string* is a directory.

-f *string* is a regular file.

-s *string* is a non-empty regular file.

-l *string* is a symbolic link.

-F *string* is a valid and accessible file.

-U *string* is a valid and accessible URL.

=*string2*
> *string* is identical to *string2*.

<*string2*
> *string* is lexicographically lower than *string2*.

>*string2*
> *string* is lexicographically greater than *string2*.

RewriteMap   mod_rewrite

`RewriteMap` *map-name map-type:map-source*

Contexts: GV

Defines a map that can be used in mapping functions within rule substitution strings. The following map types are supported:

txt:*file*
> *file* is a text file containing pairs of entries.

rnd:*file*
> *file* is a text file; each line contains a key and a sequence of values separated by a vertical bar (|), one of which will be chosen at random.

dbm:*file*
> *file* is a hashed DBM file.

---

prg:*program*

> *program* is a program that is started at server startup. It is fed a
> key as a newline-terminated string on its standard input, and is
> expected to output a value as a newline-terminated string on its
> standard output.

int:*function*

> *function* is one of the following internal functions: toupper,
> tolower, escape, or unescape.

RewriteBase   mod_rewrite

RewriteBase *url*

Contexts: SF (FileInfo)
Default: the current directory pathname

Base URL for per-directory transformations.

RewriteEngine   mod_rewrite

RewriteEngine { ON|OFF }

Contexts: GVSF (FileInfo)
Default: OFF

Enables or disables the rewriting engine.

RewriteOptions   mod_rewrite

RewriteOptions *option*

Contexts: GVSF (FileInfo)

The only option is inherit, which means virtual hosts inherit the
environment from the main server, and per-directory configuration
files inherit from their parent directory.

RewriteLock   mod_rewrite

RewriteLock *filename*

Contexts: G

Lock file to be used for synchronizing access to prg type maps.

RewriteLog

`RewriteLog` *filename*

Contexts: GV

Name of the log file for the rewriting engine.

RewriteLogLevel

`RewriteLogLevel` *digit*

Contexts: GV
Default: 0

Controls the verbosity of logging on a scale from 0 to 9. Zero disables logging while levels greater than two may be useful for debugging but will have a severe impact upon performance.

Access Restrictions

Access to documents can be restricted on the basis of the remote host, the credentials supplied (such as username and password), or other information, such as HTTP headers, attributes of the resource, or even time of day. Access controls are evaluated in three phases after URL translation. The first phase, controlled by the following directives, performs access controls that are not based on user credentials. The second and third phases authenticate the credentials and check the authenticated user against authorization rules; these phases are described in the section "Authentication and Authorization Phases."

Access Control Phase

Allow

`Allow` `from { all|`*host*`...|env=`*var* `}`

Contexts: SF* (Limit)

Specifies which hosts can access the resource according to the hostname, IP address, network/netmask specification, or setting of an environment variable. Specifying hosts by network/netmask is not supported prior to version 1.3.

Deny   mod_access

`Deny from { all|`*`host`*`...|env=`*`var`*` }`

Contexts: SF (Limit)

Specifies which hosts are denied access to a resource.

Order   mod_access

`Order { allow,deny|deny,allow|mutual-failure }`

Contexts: SF (Limit)
Default: deny,allow

Specifies the order in which allow and deny directives are evaluated.

allow,deny
   Allow directives are applied before Deny directives. Unmatched requests are denied.

deny,allow
   Deny directives are applied before Allow directives. Unmatched requests are allowed.

mutual-failure
   Only requests that match an Allow directive and are not forbidden by a Deny directive are allowed.

Authentication and Authorization Phases

Apache includes a number of standard modules to perform authentication based on information stored in text files and DB or DBM index files. These are described in this section. There are also numerous third-party modules to handle information stored in databases (such as MySQL, Oracle, or PostgreSQL) or provided by LDAP servers and so on.

Each authentication module has a directive to indicate that it is authoritative. All configured authentication modules are

---

tried in turn until one succeeds or indicates an authoritative failure.

AuthName

`AuthName` *realm-name*

Contexts: SF (AuthConfig)

Authentication realm for documents matched by the enclosing sectional directive. A realm identifies a set of resources, residing on the same server, that are protected by the same set of passwords. Note that Apache does not prevent different authentication databases from being used within the same realm.

AuthType

`AuthType` { Basic|Digest }

Contexts: SF (AuthConfig)

Type of authentication to be used.

Require

`Require` { User *user*...|Group *group*|valid user }

Contexts: SF (AuthConfig)

Specifies the authenticated users allowed to access a resource as a list of usernames or a list of groups; if the keyword valid-user is specified, any authenticated user is granted access.

Satisfy

`Satisfy` { All|Any }

Contexts: SF (AuthConfig)   *Compatibility:* 1.2 +
Default: All

The policy applied if both host-based access control and authentication are specified for a resource. Any may be used to allow non-authenticated access for requests from machines on a secure network, while requiring accesses from other hosts to be authenticated.

Authentication using text files

The simplest way to store authentication information is in plain text files; however, they are inefficient for large numbers of users and groups.

AuthAuthoritative   mod_auth

AuthAuthoritative { ON|OFF }

Contexts: SF (AuthConfig)
Default: ON

Indicates whether authentication against the user and group files is authoritative.

AuthUserFile   mod_auth

AuthUserFile *filename*

Contexts: SF (AuthConfig)

The plain text password file containing usernames and passwords. Each line consists of a username and a password field separated by colons. The passwords are encrypted with the crypt() function. Additional fields are ignored. Plain text user password files may be managed with the *htpasswd* program.

AuthGroupFile   mod_auth

AuthGroupFile *filename*

Contexts: SF (AuthConfig)

The name of the plain text file defining group membership. Each line consists of a group name followed by a colon and a space-separated list of the usernames of the members of the group.

Authentication using DB or DBM files

DB and DBM database files are simple indexed files provided on most versions of Unix. Apache provides modules supporting both variants: *mod_auth_db* and *mod_auth_dbm*. The latter module provides the same set of directives as the former, but with the abbreviation DBM embedded in the names rather than DB.

AuthDBAuthoritative

```
AuthDBAuthoritative  { ON|OFF }
```

Contexts: SF (AuthConfig)
Default: ON

If this directive is set to ON, the authentication module is authoritative.

AuthDBUserFile

```
AuthDBUserFile filename
```

Contexts: SF (AuthConfig)

Sets the path of the DB file containing usernames and passwords for authentication. The key is the username and the value contains the password encrypted with the crypt() function. The password may be followed by a colon and arbitrary data, which is ignored. DB password files may be managed with the *dbmmanage* program.

AuthDBGroupFile

```
AuthDBGroupFile filename
```

Contexts: SF (AuthConfig)

Sets the path of the DB file containing lists of user groups for authentication. The key is the username and the value contains a comma-separated list of groups to which the user belongs. Group membership may be stored in the user file by setting the group DB file to be the same as the user DB file and storing a comma-separated list of groups in the value for each user, separated from the password by a colon.

Anonymous authentication

The *mod_auth_anon* module allows anonymous authentication in a manner similar to anonymous FTP.

Anonymous

```
Anonymous user...
```

Contexts: SF (AuthConfig)

Lists *magic* usernames, which are allowed access without password verification. Note that the usernames are case-insensitive and, if enclosed in double or single quotes, may include spaces.

Anonymous_Authoritative

mod_auth_anon

```
Anonymous_Authoritative  { ON|OFF }
```

Contexts: SF (AuthConfig)
Default: OFF

If this directive is set to ON, the module is authoritative.

Anonymous_LogEmail

mod_auth_anon

```
Anonymous_LogEmail  { ON|OFF }
```

Contexts: SF (AuthConfig)
Default: ON

If this directive is set to ON, the client's password is logged to the error log.

Anonymous_MustGiveEmail

mod_auth_anon

```
Anonymous_MustGiveEmail  { ON|OFF }
```

Contexts: SF (AuthConfig)
Default: ON

If this directive is set to ON, the client must supply a non-blank password.

Anonymous_NoUserId

mod_auth_anon

```
Anonymous_NoUserId  { ON|OFF }
```

Contexts: SF (AuthConfig)
Default: OFF

If this directive is set to ON, an empty username is acceptable.

Anonymous_VerifyEmail

mod_auth_anon

```
Anonymous_VerifyEmail  { ON|OFF }
```

Contexts: SF (AuthConfig)
Default: OFF

If this directive is set to ON, the password is checked to ensure it contains an at sign (@) and a period (.); that is, that it looks at least vaguely like an email address.

MIME Type Checking Phase

The MIME typing phase occurs once access controls have been applied. It determines the content type and optionally the encoding and language of the resource. However, content generation handlers may change these attributes later.

Document Content Type

The content type of a document is used by browsers to decide how to display the document.

TypesConfig   mod_mime

`TypesConfig filename`

Contexts: G
Default: conf/mime.types

Sets the filename of the MIME types configuration file, which provides default mappings from filename extension to content type that are used if the content type is not set by other means. Blank lines in the file and lines starting with a hash sign (#) are ignored; other lines should contain a MIME type followed by zero or more extensions separated by whitespace. If the filename is not absolute, it is taken as relative to the server root directory.

DefaultType

`DefaultType MIME-type`

Contexts: GVSF (FileInfo)
Default: text/html

Sets the default content type returned for documents that cannot be typed.

AddType   mod_mime

AddType *MIME type extension...*

Contexts: GVSF* (FileInfo)

Adds a mapping from the specified extensions to the MIME type, overriding any existing mappings for the extensions.

ForceType   mod_mime

ForceType *MIME-type*

Contexts: SF (FileInfo)

Forces files to be served as the specified MIME type, regardless of file extension.

Automatic type determination

The *mod_mime_magic* module provides an alternative way of determining the content type and encoding of files. It works the same way as the Unix `file` command: it examines the first few bytes of the file and compares the data with rules specified in a *magic file*. Blank lines and comment lines starting with a hash sign (#) are ignored. Other lines define tests specified as the following fields separated by whitespace:

1. Offset in the file from which to start the next comparison. If the offset is preceded by a ">", the rule is dependent on the previous line without this prefix character.

2. Type of data to be tested; one of the following:

    byte
    > 8-bit value

    short
    > 16-bit integer value in native byte order

    long
    > 32-bit integer value in native byte order

string
> Arbitrary-length string

date
> 32-bit integer value in native byte order interpreted as a Unix date, i.e., the time since the Epoch (00:00:00 UTC, January 1, 1970), measured in seconds

beshort
> Big-endian 16-bit integer value

belong
> Big-endian 32-bit integer value

bedate
> Big-endian 32-bit integer value interpreted as a Unix date

leshort
> Little-endian 16-bit integer value

lelong
> Little-endian 32-bit integer value

ledate
> Little-endian 32-bit integer value interpreted as a Unix date

3. Value against which the data from the file should be tested

4. MIME type to use if the test succeeds

5. MIME encoding to use if the test succeeds (this field is optional)

Note that determining the content type from the magic file can degrade performance.

MimeMagicFile   mod_mime_magic

MimeMagicFile *filename*

Contexts: GV

Specifies the filename of the MIME magic file and enables the *mod_mime_magic* module. If the filename is not absolute, it is taken as relative to the server root directory.

Document Encoding

This directive specifies how documents are encoded.

AddEncoding   mod_mime

AddEncoding *MIME-encoding extension*...

Contexts: GVSF* (FileInfo)

Maps the specified extensions to the encoding type, overriding any existing mappings for the extensions. Comparison of encodings is performed ignoring any leading "x-".

Document Language and Character Set

The document language is reported to clients with the HTTP Content-language header and is also used for content selection.

AddLanguage   mod_mime

AddLanguage *MIME-language extension*...

Contexts: GVSF* (FileInfo)

Maps the specified extensions to the content language, overriding any existing mappings for any of the extensions.

DefaultLanguage   mod_mime

DefaultLanguage *MIME-language*

Contexts: GVSF (FileInfo)
Default: no default language

Specifies the default languages for files that do not have a language extension configured by the AddLanguage directive.

AddCharset   mod_mime

AddCharset *charset extension...*

Contexts: GVSF* (FileInfo)   *Compatibility:* 1.3.11 +

Maps the specified extensions to the content character set, overriding
any existing mappings for the extensions.

Generating "Expires" Headers

The optional *mod_expires* module supports the generation of
Expires headers, which inform clients, including proxies, how
long the document contents remain valid and thus how long
they may be cached. Expiration dates are given as intervals
from either the time of the access or the time the file was last
modified, and can be specified as either the letter "A" (for time
of access) or "M" (for last modified time) followed by a number of seconds, or in the format:

> *base* [plus] *number period-type...*

base may be access or now for time of access, or modifica-
tion for the last-modified time of the file. Valid period types
are years, months, weeks, days, hours, minutes, and seconds.

ExpiresActive   mod_expires

ExpiresActive { ON|OFF }

Contexts: GVSF (Indexes)

Controls whether HTTP Expires headers are generated for documents
in the matching scope.

ExpiresByType   mod_expires

ExpiresByType *MIME-type expiry-spec*

Contexts: GVSF (Indexes)

Defines how the value of Expires headers is calculated for documents
of the specified content type.

ExpiresDefault   mod_expires

ExpiresDefault *expiry-spec*

Contexts: GVSF (Indexes)

Defines how the value of Expires headers is calculated for documents that do not match any ExpiresByType directives.

Other Attributes

Apache provides a directive for enabling generation of Content-MD5 headers and two methods of providing values for other HTTP headers: either specified in the server configuration files or in separate meta-information files.

ContentDigest

ContentDigest { ON|OFF }

Contexts: GVSF (Options)   *Compatibility:* 1.1 +
Default: OFF

Enables or disables the generation of Content-MD5 headers for static documents served by the Apache core module. This header provides an integrity check but imposes a performance penalty on the server as the values are recomputed for each request.

Header   mod_headers

Header { set|append|add|unset } *header value*

Contexts: GVSF (FileInfo)

Allows arbitrary HTTP response headers to be added to, merged, or removed from the server response.

Meta-information can be stored in metafiles that contain additional HTTP headers to be returned with the responses to requests for corresponding files. Content-type and Status headers in the file are acted upon.

MetaFiles   mod_cern_meta

```
MetaFiles  { ON|OFF }
```

Contexts: GVSF (Indexes)
Default: OFF

Enables or disables metafile processing.

MetaDir   mod_cern_meta

```
MetaDir  dir-name
```

Contexts: GVSF (Indexes)
Default: .web

Name of the subdirectory containing meta-information files.

MetaSuffix   mod_cern_meta

```
MetaSuffix  suffix
```

Contexts: GVSF (Indexes)
Default: .meta

Filename suffix for meta-information files.

Content Generation Phase

Apache offers many ways of generating content:

Static files
    Contained in static files

As-is files
    Static files containing complete responses including HTTP headers

Negotiated content
    Selected according to client preferences

Directory indexes
    Generated listings of directory contents

Imagemaps
Selected according to where the user clicks on an image

Proxy requests
Retrieved from another HTTP server, proxy, or FTP server

CGI scripts
Generated by an external program

Server-side includes
HTML files containing embedded directives that are expanded when the request is processed

Server status and information
Automatically generated real-time status pages

Customized error responses
Custom error documents

Third-party modules
Many types of content generated using the Apache API

Handlers

Handlers are named, internal functions that generate content. How the content is generated is determined according to the handler or the MIME type that has been set for the resource. If no handler is specified, a default handler is used that simply sends the contents of a file as the response. The following table lists the standard Apache handlers.

Handler Name	Description
cgi-script	Content generated by a CGI script.
default-handler	Static content.
imap-file	Imagemap rule file.
perl-script	Content generated by a *mod_perl* script.
send-as-is	File includes HTTP headers and is sent as-is.
server-info	Generated server configuration information page.
server-parsed	Server-side include file.

Handler Name	Description
server-status	Generated server status page.
type-map	Content selection type map.

The following directives control the association of handlers to filename extensions.

AddHandler   mod_mime

AddHandler *handler-name extension*...

Contexts: GVSF* (FileInfo)   *Compatibility:* 1.1 +

Associates the named handler with the filename extensions specified. Any existing association for any of the extensions is overridden.

RemoveHandler   mod_mime

RemoveHandler *extension*...

Contexts: SF (FileInfo)   *Compatibility:* 1.3.4 +

Removes the handler association for the specified extensions.

SetHandler   mod_mime

SetHandler *handler-name*

Contexts: SF (FileInfo)   *Compatibility:* 1.1 +

Associates all files in the current scope with the specified handler, regardless of the extension.

Content-Negotiated Documents

Content negotiation, controlled by the following directives, allows the best variant of a resource that is available in multiple representations to be selected according to the values of the Accept-* HTTP request headers. The available variants may be determined automatically if the requested resource does not exist and the MultiViews option is enabled for the directory. Variants and their attributes may alternatively be specified explicitly in a type map file if the requested URI is for the type map file and the handler is set to type-map.

A type map file contains a number of stanzas comprising header records that define the attributes (Content-Encoding, Content-Language, Content-Length, and Content-Type) for a variant. The URI header gives the path of the variant relative to the map file.

CacheNegotiatedDocs   mod_negotiation

CacheNegotiatedDocs

Contexts: GV

Allows content-negotiated documents to be cached by proxies.

LanguagePriority   mod_negotiation

LanguagePriority *MIME-language*...

Contexts: GVSF (FileInfo)

Sets the precedence in decreasing order for language variants for when a document is selected by MultiViews and the client does not specify a preference with the HTTP Accept-Language header.

Directory Indexes

When a request is received for a URL that maps to a directory, Apache can return a file named in the DirectoryIndex directive or can automatically generate a listing.

DirectoryIndex   mod_dir

DirectoryIndex *file*...

Contexts: GVSF* (Indexes)
Default: index.html

Lists resources to look for when a request maps to a directory name. If none of the resources can be found and the Indexes feature of the Options directive is enabled, a directory listing will be generated.

Automatically generated directory indexes

If there is no index file for a directory and the `Indexes` feature of the `Options` directive is enabled, a directory listing will be generated. This may be a plain list of filenames or a *fancy index*, in which by default each line consists of an icon containing the file type, the filename, the time the file was last modified, the file size, and a description of the file.

IndexOptions   mod_autoindex

`IndexOptions [+|-]option...`

Contexts: GVSF (Indexes)
Default: no options

Controls the formatting of automatically generated directory indexes. The following options are recognized:

`DescriptionWidth={n| * }`
> Sets the width of the description column. If specified as an asterisk (*), indicates the width of the longest description. (1.3.11 +)

`FancyIndexing`
> Enables fancy indexing.

`FoldersFirst`
> Causes subdirectories to be listed before files. (1.3.11 +)

`IconsAreLinks`
> Makes each icon a link to the file listed on that line.

`IconHeight=pixels`
> If this option is specified, a `HEIGHT` attribute is generated for the `IMG` element for each icon, allowing browsers to calculate the layout of the page before all the images have been downloaded. (1.3 +)

`IconWidth=pixels`
> If this option is specified, a `WIDTH` attribute is generated for the `IMG` element for each icon. (1.3 +)

`NameWidth=n`
> Specifies the width of the filename column in bytes. If *n* is specified as an asterisk (*), the column is automatically sized to the length of the longest filename.

ScanHTMLTitles
> Scans HTML files for TITLE tags and uses the values as the file descriptions.

SuppressColumnSorting
> Disables the generation of sortable listings.

SuppressDescription
> Suppresses the file description column.

SuppressHTMLPreamble
> If a header file is specified with the HeaderName and the file contains a valid HTML header, the generated header will be suppressed and instead taken from the header file.

SuppressLastModified
> Suppresses the last-modified date and time column.

SuppressSize
> Suppresses the file size column.

IndexOrderDefault   mod_autoindex

IndexOrderDefault *sort-order field-name*

Contexts: GVSF (Indexes)   *Compatibility:* 1.3.4 +
Default: files are sorted in ascending order by filename

Specifies how files should be ordered within the directory listing. *sort-order* may be Ascending or Descending, and *field-name* may be Name, Date, Size, or Description.

IndexIgnore   mod_autoindex

IndexIgnore *pattern*...

Contexts: GVSF* (Indexes)

Specifies files to be excluded from the directory listing.

HeaderName   mod_autoindex

HeaderName *filename*

Contexts: GVSF (Indexes)

Names the file containing descriptive header text that is inserted at the top of the directory listing. If this is an HTML file, and the SuppressHTMLPreamble index option is specified, the appearance of the

---

index can be influenced by BODY attributes, such as BACKGROUND or BGCOLOR.

ReadmeName
mod_autoindex

ReadmeName *filename*

Contexts: GVSF (Indexes)

Names the file appended to the end of the directory listing.

The remaining directives control the appearance of the lines of fancy indexes that describe files, that is, the icons that are used, the alternative text for the icons, and the descriptions of the files.

DefaultIcon
mod_autoindex

DefaultIcon *url*

Contexts: GVSF (Indexes)

Specifies the relative URL of the icon to display when no other icon is associated with a file's type or encoding.

AddIcon
mod_autoindex

AddIcon { *url*|*alt,url* } *file*...

Contexts: GVSF* (Indexes)

Specifies the relative URL, or ALT text and URL, of the icon to display for files matching the names given. *file* can be a filename extension, a wildcard expression, a partial or complete filename, the string `^^DIRECTORY^^` for directories, or `^^BLANKICON^^` for the blank icon used to line up the columns.

AddIconByType
mod_autoindex

AddIconByType { *url*|*alt,url* } *MIME-type*...

Contexts: GVSF* (Indexes)

Specifies the relative URL of the icon to display for files whose MIME type matches one of those listed.

AddIconByEncoding   mod_autoindex

AddIconByEncoding { *url|alt,url* } *MIME-encoding*...

Contexts: GVSF* (Indexes)

Specifies the relative URL of the icon to display for files whose MIME encoding matches one of those listed.

The following directives control the value of the ALT attribute for the icons that are included in the listing.

AddAlt   mod_autoindex

AddAlt "*string*" *filename*...

Contexts: GVSF* (Indexes)

Sets the value of the ALT attribute for the icon images included for files that match *filename*.

AddAltByEncoding   mod_autoindex

AddAltByEncoding "*string*" *MIME-encoding*...

Contexts: GVSF* (Indexes)

Sets the value of the ALT attribute for the icon images included for files with the specified encoding.

AddAltByType   mod_autoindex

AddAltByType "*string*" *MIME-type*...

Contexts: GVSF* (Indexes)

Sets the value of the ALT attribute for the icon images included for files with the specified content type.

The following directive controls the descriptive text displayed.

AddDescription   mod_autoindex

AddDescription "*description*" *file-pattern*...

Contexts: GVSF* (Indexes)

Sets the descriptive text to display for a file.

Imagemaps

Imagemaps define mappings between regions of an image, marked in an HTML document with the ISMAP attribute, and link destinations. Client-side imagemaps are handled entirely by the user agent. Server-side maps cause the user agent to issue a GET request for the URL specified in the enclosing HTML A element; the x and y coordinates of the point clicked are passed as the query string value.

Imagemaps are set up on the server by associating a handler of imap-file with a map file. The coordinates supplied by the user agent are compared against rules specified in the map file, which may take the following forms:

base *url*
> Base URL for relative URLs in the map file (overrides the ImapBase directive).

default ["*text*"]
> Action to take if the coordinates do not fall within any of the defined regions and there are no defined points.

circle *action* ["*text*"] *x1,y1 x2,y2* ["*text*"]
> Defines a circular region specified by the coordinates of the center and a point on the circumference.

poly *action* ["*text*"] *x1,y1 x2,y2 x3,y3* ... ["*text*"]
> Defines a polygonal region specified by the coordinates of the vertices. Between 3 and 100 vertices may be specified.

rect *action* ["*text*"] *x1,y1 x2,y2* ["*text*"]
> Defines a rectangular region specified by the coordinates of two opposing corners.

point *action* ["*text*"] *x,y* ["*text*"]
> If the selected point falls outside any of the areas defined with circle, poly, and rect directives, the closest point is taken.

The quoted text is used as the text of the link if a menu is generated. It may appear before or after the coordinates.

The possible actions are described in the following table.

Action	Description
url	Destination URL of the link—either absolute or relative to the base value
map	Generates an HTML index unless ImapMenu is set to None
menu	Synonymous with map
referer	Equivalent to the URL of the referring document or to the URL of the server if the request did not contain a Referer header
nocontent	Sends a response with status 204 (no content) that tells the client to continue to display the same page (not valid for base)
error	Sends an error response with status 500 (server error)

ImapBase   mod_imap

ImapBase { map|referer|*url* }

Contexts: GVSF (Indexes)   *Compatibility:* 1.1 +
Default: scheme://server/

Base URL for the imagemap. The default uses the current scheme (http, https, ftp, etc) on the current server. May be overridden by a base directive in the map file.

ImapDefault   mod_imap

ImapDefault { error|nocontent|referer|menu|*url* }

Contexts: GVSF (Indexes)   *Compatibility:* 1.1 +
Default: nocontent

The default action for the imagemap. May be overridden by a default directive in the map file.

ImapMenu   mod_imap

ImapMenu { none|formatted|semiformatted|unformatted }

Contexts: GVSF (Indexes)   *Compatibility:* 1.1 +

The action to be taken if the request for an imagemap file does not contain valid coordinates.

Proxy/Cache Directives

The *mod_proxy* module adds proxy server and caching capabilities to Apache, allowing documents to be fetched from remote servers (which themselves may be proxy servers). In practice, it may be better to deploy a dedicated proxy cache server such as Squid (*http://www.squid-cache.org*).

A request is deemed to be a proxy request if the hostname in the URL is not one served by the server. Proxy requests are flagged as such during the first phase of request processing by prefixing the URL with the string proxy:. Directory and location sections that apply to proxied URLs should match against the prefixed URL. Requests can be rewritten to be proxy requests by the *mod_rewrite* module.

ProxyRequests   mod_proxy

ProxyRequests { ON|OFF }

Contexts: GV
Default. OFF

Enables or disables the proxy module.

ProxyPass   mod_proxy

ProxyPass *path url*

Contexts: GV*

Maps the remote URL into the local server's namespace, making the proxy appear to be a mirror of the remote server. This is known as *reverse proxying*.

ProxyPassReverse   mod_proxy

ProxyPassReverse *path url*

Contexts: GV*

Adjusts Location headers on redirect responses when acting as a reverse proxy, to avoid the client becoming aware that resources are mirrored.

AllowCONNECT   mod_proxy

AllowCONNECT *port*...

Contexts: GV
Default: 443 and 563

Specifies the remote ports that may be used in CONNECT requests.

ProxyBlock   mod_proxy

ProxyBlock { **|host|domain* } ...

Contexts: GV*

Blocks requests for documents from sites that contain any of the items specified in the list. Any items that may be DNS names are looked up when the server starts and the corresponding IP addresses are added to the list.

ProxyDomain   mod_proxy

ProxyDomain *domain-name*

Contexts: GV

When a request is received that contains an unqualified hostname, this causes a redirection response to the same host with this *domain name* appended. This is useful only if the server is serving an intranet.

ProxyRemote   mod_proxy

ProxyRemote *url-prefix remote-server*

Contexts: GV*

Specifies a remote proxy that should be contacted for requests matching *url-prefix*, which may be a partial URL, a URL scheme for which the remote proxy should be used, or an asterisk (*) to indicate that the remote proxy should be used for all proxy requests.

NoProxy

NoProxy { *host*|*domain*|*ip-addr*|*subnet* } ...

Contexts: GV*

Causes requests for documents from the specified sites to be served directly and not forwarded to a proxy server configured with the ProxyRemote directive.

ProxyVia

ProxyVia { ON|OFF|Full|Block }

Contexts: GV   *Compatibility:* 1.3.2 +
Default: OFF

Controls the processing of Via headers as follows:

ON   A Via header is generated for the current host, and Via header
     lines in requests and replies are not modified.

OFF No Via headers are generated, but Via header lines in requests
     and replies are left in place.

Full
     A Via header is generated for the current host, with the Apache
     server version included as a comment field. Existing Via header
     lines in requests and replies are not modified.

Block
     No Via headers are generated, and Via header lines in requests
     and replies are removed.

ProxyReceiveBufferSize

ProxyReceiveBufferSize *number-bytes*

Contexts: GV

Allows the system's network buffer size to be adjusted from the default size to improve throughput.

Caching

The *mod_proxy* module can cache documents that are retrieved from remote servers, thus saving network bandwidth and improving response times for subsequent requests. Caching is enabled by setting the pathname of the top-level cache directory.

Responses are stored in files in the cache directory hierarchy, the names of which are formed from a hash of the URI. The cache is structured as a hierarchy of directories to reduce the number of files in each directory and so reduce the time taken for directory searches. The cache is pruned periodically by a garbage collector to prevent it from growing indefinitely.

CacheRoot   mod_proxy

CacheRoot *directory*

Contexts: GV

Specifies the pathname of the top-level cache directory.

CacheDirLevels   mod_proxy

CacheDirLevels *number*

Contexts: GV
Default: 3

Specifies the number of levels in the cache directory hierarchy.

CacheDirLength   mod_proxy

CacheDirLength *number*

Contexts: GV
Default: 1

Specifies the length of subdirectory names.

CacheSize   mod_proxy

CacheSize *kb*

Contexts: GV
Default: 5

Specifies the nominal size of the the cache. The garbage collector periodically deletes files from the cache to reduce the size to this value.

CacheGcInterval   mod_proxy

CacheGcInterval *hours*

Contexts: GV

Specifies the period in hours between runs of the garbage collector.

CacheForceCompletion   mod_proxy

CacheForceCompletion *percentage-complete*

Contexts: GV   *Compatibility:* 1.3.1 +
Default: 90

Specifies the threshold above which the server will continue to transfer documents to cache if the transfer is canceled.

NoCache   mod_proxy

NoCache { *|*host*|*domain* } ...

Contexts: GV*

Specifies that requests containing words, hosts, or domains from the list will not be cached.

CacheDefaultExpire   mod_proxy

CacheDefaultExpire *hours*

Contexts: GV
Default: 1

Specifies the expiry time used for documents retrieved using a protocol that does not support expiry times.

CacheLastModifiedFactor   mod_proxy

CacheLastModifiedFactor *factor*

Contexts: GV
Default: 0.1

Specifies that if a retrieved document does not have an expiration date, one should be calculated by multiplying the age of the document (as indicated by the Last-Modified header) by this factor.

CacheMaxExpire   mod_proxy

CacheMaxExpire *hours*

Contexts: GV
Default: 24

Specifies the maximum period before the server will check with the remote server that a cached document is still valid.

CGI Scripts

The CGI interface allows applications to be launched from web servers in a way that is language-independent and portable between most web servers. The downside is the overhead required to launch the CGI script for each request. Embedded interpreters, such as *mod_perl*, avoid this overhead and provide better performance. Other solutions such as FastCGI and SpeedyCGI provide a CGI-like environment in a separate process and also avoid most of this overhead.

Files are regarded as CGI scripts if the handler is set to cgi-script, and are executed in accordance with the CGI specification. If the *suEXEC* CGI wrapper is properly installed, Apache will run scripts as the user and group specified for a virtual host, or as the owner of a user-specific directory. Otherwise, they will be run as the user and group under which the web server child processes run.

Action   mod_actions

Action { *MIME-type|handler-name* } *script*

Contexts: GVSF* (FileInfo)

Specifies the script to be invoked if the MIME type or handler matches that of the requested resource.

`Script` *method script*

Contexts: GVS

Specifies the script to be invoked if the HTTP request method is that given.

Environment variables

Apache sets up the standard CGI environment variables and additional variables listed in the section "CGI Environment Variables." In addition, variables can be passed from the environment the server inherits from the invoking shell, controlled by the following directives.

PassEnv mod_env

`PassEnv` *varname...*

Contexts: GV*   *Compatibility:* 1.1 +

Specifies variables to be passed from the server's environment to that of the CGI script.

SetEnv mod_env

`SetEnv` *varname value*

Contexts: GV*   *Compatibility:* 1.1 +

Sets the environment variable to the specified value and places it in the environment of the CGI script.

UnsetEnv mod_env

`UnsetEnv` *varname...*

Contexts: GV   *Compatibility:* 1.1 +

Removes the specified variables from the environment of the CGI script.

Script logging

The script logging feature aids the debugging of CGI scripts by collecting the request header fields, any error messages, the response, and all output in one log file.

ScriptLog   mod_cgi

ScriptLog *filename*

Contexts: G

Specifies the name of the CGI script error log file. Without this directive no log file is created.

ScriptLogBuffer   mod_cgi

ScriptLogBuffer *size-bytes*

Contexts: G
Default: 1,024

Specifies the maximum size of a PUT or POST entity body that is logged without truncation.

ScriptLogLength   mod_cgi

ScriptLogLength *length-bytes*

Contexts: G
Default: 10,385,760

Specifies the maximum length of the script log file. No more information is logged to the file once this size is reached.

Server-Side Includes (SSI)

Server-side include documents are HTML documents interpreted by the server, containing the following commands embedded within HTML comments:

<!--#config [*attribute=value*]... -->

Configures aspects of parsing. Valid attributes are:

---

errmsg
>   Message returned if an error occurs during SSI parsing.

sizefmt
>   Format to use for file sizes; either bytes or abbrev.

timefmt
>   strftime() format string used for dates.

`<!--#echo encoding={url|none}var=var -->`
>   Prints the value of a CGI or SSI variable specified with the var attribute (see the section "CGI Environment Variables" for a list of variables). The encoding attribute is new in version 1.3.12.

`<!--#set var=varname value=value -->`
>   Sets the value of the variable specified.

`<!--#printenv -->`
>   Prints a list of all variables and their values.

`<!--#exec {cmd=cmd-string|cgi=url-path } -->`
>   Executes the shell command (using /bin/sh) or the CGI script specified.

`<!--#fsize {file=file-path|virtual=url-path} -->`
>   Prints the size of the file specified.

`<!--#flastmod {file=file-path|virtual=url-path } -->`
>   Prints the last modification time of the file specified.

`<!--#include {file=file-path|virtual=url-path } -->`
>   Includes the file specified.

`<!--#if expr="cond" -->`
`<!--#elif expr="cond" -->`
`<!--#else -->`
`<!--#endif -->`
>   Defines conditional blocks. The following comparison operators are supported: =, !=, <, <=, <, and >=. Comparisons may be enclosed in parentheses for grouping, prefixed by an exclamation point (!) to negate the condition, and combined with AND (&&) or OR (||) operators.

CGI and SSI variables may be interpolated into quoted strings by prefixing the variable name with a dollar sign ($). The name must be enclosed within curly braces to delimit it, if followed by valid name characters.

The files must have the handler set as `server-parsed` to be interpreted, and the option `Includes` must be enabled for the directory containing the file. The `IncludesNOEXEC` option disables the `exec` command and any file inclusion that would result in the execution of a CGI script. The `XBitHack` directive provides an alternative method of flagging server-parsed HTML documents.

XBitHack   mod_include

`XBitHack  { ON|OFF|Full }`

Contexts: GVSF (Options)
Default: OFF

Controls parsing of files with content type `text/html`. If this directive is set to `ON` or `Full`, files that have the user-execute bit set are treated as server-parsed HTML documents. If it is set to `Full` and the group-execute bit is set, a `Last-Modified` HTTP response header will be sent with the last-modified time of the file.

Server-Generated Status Pages

The server information page provides an overview of the server configuration, including all installed modules and directives. It is generated by the `server-info` handler.

AddModuleInfo   mod_info

`AddModuleInfo` *module text*

Contexts: GV*

Adds the HTML string to the *Additional Information* section of the server information display.

The status page is generated by the `server-status` handler and provides an overview of the server configuration.

ExtendedStatus mod_status

ExtendedStatus { ON|OFF }

Contexts: G
Default: OFF

Controls whether minimal or detailed statistics are maintained for display as a status page. Enabling extended statistics imposes a small performance penalty, as additional statistics must be collected.

Note that if active, the *mod_info* and *mod_status* modules will be available in per-directory configuration files, so users with control over those files will be able to publish information about the server.

Customized Error Responses

Apache allows the normal hardcoded error response to be replaced with customized responses.

ErrorDocument

ErrorDocument *error-code* { "*message|url*" }

Contexts: GVSF (FileInfo)

Configures the response Apache generates for error responses. The response document can be a message string indicated by a double quote character (") or the URL of a local or external document. If the local URL refers to a CGI script or SSI document, details of the request can be extracted from the environment. Note that any trailing quote will be taken as part of the message.

Request Logging Phase

The last phase of request processing is request logging. The standard logging module, *mod_log_config*, superceded the *mod_log_common* module in Apache version 1.2. It can replace cookie and referrer logs with its more generalized facilities. Log entry format strings contain literal text interspersed with format specifiers, described in this table.

Specifier	Description
%a	Remote IP address
%B	Bytes sent, or "-" if zero (1.3.11 +)
%b	Number of bytes sent (excluding headers)
%{*var*}e	Environment variable *var*
%f	Filename
%H	Request protocol(1.3.11 +)
%h	Remote host
%{*hdr*}i	Value of incoming header *hdr*
%l	Remote logname from identd (if enabled)
%m	Request method (1.3.11 +)
%{*label*}n	Labelled note from another module
%{*hdr*}o	Value of outgoing header *hdr*
%p	Canonical port number of the server
%P	Process ID of the child process serving the request
%q	Query string (1.3.11 +)
%r	First line of the request
%s	Request status
%t	Time in Common Log Format (CLF) format
%{*fmt*}t	Time formatted according to *fmt*, a strftime() format
%T	Time taken to process the request
%u	Authenticated remote username
%U	URL requested
%v	Canonical server name of the server
%V	Server name according to the setting of the UseCanonicalName directive

If the *mod_unique_id* module is active, the unique identifier for the request can be included with %{UNIQUE_ID}e. Cookies generated by the *mod_usertrack* module can be included with %{cookie}n. Request logging is controlled by the following directives. Note that the cookie is set during the fix-up phase.

LogFormat

mod_log_config

LogFormat *format-string[format-name]*

Contexts: GV*

Without a *format-name*, sets the format for log files created with subsequent TransferLog directives. With a *format-name*, creates a named format that can be used in CustomLog directives. *format-string* describes the format of each log line.

CustomLog

mod_log_config

CustomLog *file-or-pipe* { *format-string* | *format-name* }
[env=[!]*var*]

Contexts: GV*   *Compatibility:* 1.3 +

Adds the named log file using the specified format string or named format. Logging may be conditional if the optional last argument is specified.

TransferLog

mod_log_config

TransferLog *file-or-pipe*

Contexts: GV*
Default: logs/access_log

Adds the named log using the format defined by the most recent LogFormat directive.

CookieTracking

mod_usertrack

CookieTracking { ON | OFF }

Contexts: GVSF (FileInfo)
Default: OFF

Enables user tracking by sending a cookie for each new request.

CookieExpires

mod_usertrack

CookieExpires *expiry-period*

Contexts: GV

Sets the expiration period on user-tracking cookies, either as a number of seconds or as a string such as "1 hour 30 minutes".

CookieName   mod_usertrack

CookieName *token*

Contexts: GVSF (FileInfo)
Default: Apache

Specifies the name of the user-tracking cookie, consisting of letters, digits, underscores (_), and hyphens (-).

strftime( ) Time Formats

Date and time format specifiers defined by the strftime() function are used in log format strings and server-side includes configuration options. Ordinary characters in the format string are copied literally. Conversion specifiers are introduced by a percent sign (%), and are interpreted as shown in the following table.

Spec.	Description
%a	Abbreviated name of the day of the week
%A	Full name of the day of the week
%b	Abbreviated month name according to the current locale
%B	Full month name according to the current locale
%c	Preferred date and time representation for the current locale
%d	Two-digit day of the month (01–31)
%H	Two-digit hour using the 24-hour clock (01–23)
%I	Two-digit hour using the 12-hour clock (01–12)
%j	Three-digit day of the year (001–366)
%M	Two-digit minutes (00–59)
%m	Two-digit month number (01–12)
%p	Current locale's 12-hour clock A.M./P.M. indicator
%S	Seconds (00–61, to allow for leap seconds)
%U	Two-digit week number (00–53, where weeks start on a Sunday and week 1 is the first full week of the year)

Spec.	Description
%W	Two-digit week number (00–53, where weeks start on a Monday and week 1 is the first full week of the year)
%w	Day of the week (0–6, where 0 represents Sunday)
%X	Preferred time representation for the current locale (without the date)
%x	Preferred date representation for the current locale (without the time)
%Y	Year as a four-digit number (including the century)
%y	Year as a two-digit number (without the century)
%Z	Time zone abbreviation

Secure Versions of Apache

Secure versions of Apache add support for SSL/TLS (Secure Socket Layer and Transport Layer Security), which provides the ability to encrypt all data exchanged between the client and server, and to authenticate the server to the client and vice versa.

There are two open source secure versions of Apache: Apache-SSL and *mod_ssl* (which is derived from Apache-SSL). Both use the OpenSSL library, which is the successor to SSLeay. Of the commercial versions of Apache, Red Hat Secure Web Server and the Covalent Raven SSL Module use *mod_ssl*. C2Net's Stronghold is derived from an earlier implementation called Sioux, and IBM HTTP Server uses a proprietary implementation of SSL. This situation is confusing because the different versions often have different names for the same or similar directives. The directive compatibility summary lines in this section list the versions of secure Apache to which the directive refers (IBM HTTP Server is abbreviated as IHS). Version numbers indicate the first version of the server that supports the directive.

Note that name-based virtual hosts do not work with secure versions of Apache, because the hostname of the virtual host, taken from the Host HTTP header, is required to locate the appropriate server certificate to set up the connection, but this hostname is not available until after the secure connection has been established.

Secure Server Options

SSLEngine

SSLEngine { ON|OFF }

Contexts: GV   *Compatibility:* mod_ssl 2.1
Default: OFF

Enables or disables the operation of the SSL/TLS protocol engine.

SSLDisable

SSLDisable

Contexts: GV   *Compatibility:* Apache-SSL, IHS

Disables the operation of the SSL/TLS protocol engine.

SSLEnable

SSLEnable

Contexts: GV   *Compatibility:* Apache-SSL, IHS

Enables the operation of the SSL/TLS protocol engine.

SSLFlag

SSLFlag { ON|OFF }

Contexts: GV   *Compatibility:* Stronghold
Default: OFF

Enables or disables the operation of the SSL/TLS protocol engine.

SSLRoot

SSLRoot *directory*

Contexts: GV   *Compatibility:* Stronghold

Specifies the root directory for relative SSL-related filenames (other than the SSL log file).

SSLOptions

SSLOptions [+|-]*option*...

Contexts: GVSF (Options)   *Compatibility:* mod_ssl 2.1

Sets various runtime options. The available options are:

StdEnvVars
> Enables the creation of SSL-related CGI/SSI environment variables. Disabled by default for performance reasons.

CompatEnvVars
> Enables additional SSL-related CGI/SSI environment variables for compatibility with other secure versions of Apache.

ExportCertData
> Creates additional CGI/SSI environment variables to hold the PEM encoded client and server certificates for the current connection. This is disabled by default, as the amount of information put into the environment can exceed the operating system limit and make it impossible to start CGI scripts.

FakeBasicAuth
> The Subject Distinguished Name of the client's certificate is taken as the HTTP Basic Authentication username, so that standard authorization methods can be used. No password is obtained from the user, but a password of xxj31ZMTZzkVA (the word *password* encrypted) is assumed and should be placed in the user password file.

StrictRequire
> Overrides a Satisfy Any setting, so that access control failure by *mod_ssl* is authoritative.

OptRenegotiate
> Optimizes SSL connection renegotiation.

SSLFakeBasicAuth

SSLFakeBasicAuth

Contexts: G   *Compatibility:* Apache-SSL, IHS, Stronghold

Identical to *mod_ssl*'s SSLOptions FakeBasicAuth option.

SSLExportClientCertificates

SSLExportClientCertificates

Contexts: G   *Compatibility:* Apache-SSL

Similar to *mod_ssl*'s SSLOptions ExportCertData option.

SSLPassPhraseDialog

SSLPassPhraseDialog { builtin|exec:*program* }

Contexts: G   *Compatibility:* mod_ssl 2.1

Specifies the type of dialogue (built-in or through an external program) to employ for getting the passphrases for encrypted private key files.

SSLV2Timeout

SSLV2Timeout *secs*

Contexts: G   *Compatibility:* IHS
Default: 40

Specifies the timeout for an SSL version 2 session. Once the timeout expires, another SSL handshake is performed.

SSLV3Timeout

SSLV3Timeout *secs*

Contexts: G   *Compatibility:* IHS
Default: 120

Specifies the timeout for an SSL version 3 session.

SSLRandomSeed

SSLRandomSeed { startup|connect } *source* [*bytes*]

Contexts: G*   *Compatibility:* mod_ssl 2.2

Configures sources (described in the following table) for seeding the pseudo-random number generator during server startup or as a new SSL connection is established.

Source	Description
builtin	Internal function that uses the current time, process ID, and an extract of the Apache scoreboard data to seed the generator.
file:*name*	External file, such as the kernel random number source devices.
exec:*prog*	External program. Note that this source is not recommended for use with connect.

SSLRandomFile

SSLRandomFile *filename bytes*

Contexts: G*   *Compatibility:* Apache-SSL 1.31

Specifies the source of random bytes that are read at server startup.

SSLRandomFilePerConnection

SSLRandomFilePerConnection *filename bytes*

Contexts. G*   *Compatibility:* Apache-SSL

Specifies the source of random bytes that are read when a new session is being negotiated.

StrongholdLicenseFile

StrongholdLicenseFile *filename*

Contexts: GV   *Compatibility:* Stronghold

Specifies the filename of the Stronghold license file.

Certificates

Certificates contain the subject's public key, information about the certificate, the identity of the subject and of the issuer (certificate authority, or CA), and a digital signature that is a checksum of the information in the certificate encrypted with the issuer's private key. The validity of the signature can be checked by calculating the checksum and comparing it with the signature decrypted with the issuer's public key. If the issuing CA's certificate is available, it is used to authenticate

---

the subject. Use of the subject's public key from the certificate enables data to be encrypted so that it can be decrypted only by the holder of the corresponding private key, ensuring secure communication.

Server certificate

The server certificate, controlled by the following directives, is used for client-side authentication of the server.

SSLCertificateFile

SSLCertificateFile *filename*

Contexts: GV   *Compatibility:* mod_ssl 2.0, Apache-SSL, Stronghold

Specifies the file containing the PEM-encoded certificate for the server. The file may also contain the private key, which may be encrypted, in which case a passphrase will be requested at server startup (does not apply to Stronghold).

SSLCertificateKeyFile

SSLCertificateKeyFile *filename*

Contexts: GV   *Compatibility:* mod_ssl 2.0, Apache-SSL, Stronghold

Specifies the file containing the PEM-encoded private key for the server (if the private key is not combined with the certificate).

KeyFile

KeyFile *filename*

Contexts: G   *Compatibility:* IHS

Specifies the file containing server certificates.

SSLServerCert

SSLServerCert *certificate-label*

Contexts: G   *Compatibility:* IHS
Default: first certificate in keyfile

Specifies the label of the server certificate to use.

Certificate authority certificates

Certificates for trusted CAs are used to verify client certificates presented to the server.

SSLCACertificateFile

`SSLCACertificateFile` *filename*

Contexts: GV   *Compatibility:* mod_ssl 2.0, Apache-SSL, Stronghold

Specifies the file containing concatenated PEM-encoded certificates of CAs whose client certificates are used for client authentication.

SSLCACertificatePath

`SSLCACertificatePath` *directory*

Contexts: GV   *Compatibility:* mod_ssl 2.0, Apache-SSL, Stronghold

Specifies the directory containing encoded certificates of CAs whose client certificates are used for client authentication. The files containing each certificate are accessed through hash filenames.

SSLCertificateChainFile

`SSLCertificateChainFile` *filename*

Contexts: GV   *Compatibility:* mod_ssl 2.3

Specifies the file containing the certificates of the CAs that form the certificate chain of the server certificate. The certificates stored in this file will not be used for client authentication unless they are also present in the CA certificate file or path.

SSLNoCAList

`SSLNoCAList`

Contexts: GV   *Compatibility:* Apache-SSL 1.3.6

Disables the presentation of CA list for client certificate authentication. Useful only for testing.

Certificate Revocation Lists (CRLs)

Certificate Revocation Lists (CRLs) are lists of certificates, signed by the CA, that are no longer valid.

SSLCARevocationFile

`SSLCARevocationFile filename`

Contexts: GV   *Compatibility:* mod_ssl 2.3

Specifies the file containing the concatenation of all PEM-encoded CRLs of trusted CAs.

SSLCARevocationPath

`SSLCARevocationPath directory`

Contexts: GV   *Compatibility:* mod_ssl 2.3

Directory containing PEM-encoded CRL files of trusted CAs. The names of the files in this directory are hash values.

Proxy certificate authentication

Proxy certificate authentication is a feature currently offered only by Stronghold. When Stronghold acts as a mirror proxy for an SSL server, it makes an SSL connection to that server and may be asked for a client certificate. It receives a list of CAs that are acceptable and selects a certificate that matches.

SSLProxyMachineCertFile

`SSLProxyMachineCertFile filename`

Contexts: GV   *Compatibility:* Stronghold

Specifies the file containing certificates to present for authentication with a remote server.

SSLProxyMachineCertPath

`SSLProxyMachineCertPath directory`

Contexts: GV   *Compatibility:* Stronghold

Specifies the directory containing certificates to present for authentication with a remote server.

SSLProxyCACertificateFile

`SSLProxyCACertificateFile` *filename*

Contexts: GV   *Compatibility:* Stronghold

Specifies the file containing certificates for CAs for authenticating the origin server.

SSLProxyCACertificatePath

`SSLProxyCACertificatePath` *directory*

Contexts: GV   *Compatibility:* Stronghold

Specifies the directory containing certificates for CAs used for authenticating the origin server.

SSLProxyVerifyDepth

`SSLProxyVerifyDepth` *number*

Contexts: GV   *Compatibility:* Stronghold

Sets the number of CAs to be followed in the chain of CA certificates when verifying a remote server's certificate.

Session Caching

Each of the secure Apache servers provides a mechanism to cache session keys for reuse so as to avoid unnecessary session handshakes when a client requests multiple documents in parallel. However, each server uses completely different directives, as described in the following sections.

The mod_ssl server

The following directives are specific to this server.

SSLSessionCache

`SSLSessionCache` { none | dbm:*filename* | shm:*filename*[*size*] }

Contexts: G   *Compatibility:* mod_ssl 2.1
Default: none

Specifies the interprocess SSL session cache DBM file.

SSLSessionCacheTimeout

`SSLSessionCacheTimeout` *seconds*

Contexts: GV   *Compatibility:* mod_ssl 2.0
Default: 300

Sets the timeout in seconds for the information stored in the interprocess SSL session cache file.

SSLMutex

`SSLMutex { none|sem|file:`*filename*` }`

Contexts: G   *Compatibility:* mod_ssl 2.1
Default: none

Specifies the type of lock mechanism used for serializing operations that have to be synchronized, such as access to the session cache.

Lock Type	Description
none	No locking performed. Not recommended.
sem	Uses a semaphore under Unix or a mutex under Win32. This lock type provides the best performance if the operating system supports it.
file:*name*	Physical lock file. Most portable method.

The Apache-SSL server

The following directives are specific to this server.

SSLCacheServerPath

`SSLCacheServerPath` *filename*

Contexts: G   *Compatibility:* Apache-SSL

Sets the path of the global cache server program, `gcache`. The path may be absolute or relative to the server root directory.

SSLCacheServerPort

`SSLCacheServerPort  { port-number|filename }`

Contexts: G   *Compatibility:* Apache-SSL 1.27

Sets the port number of the TCP/IP port or filename of the Unix domain socket on which the global cache server listens for connections.

SSLCacheServerRunDir

`SSLCacheServerRunDir directory`

Contexts: G   *Compatibility:* Apache-SSL

Specifies the directory to which the cache server changes and where any *core* files will be created.

Stronghold

Stronghold stores sessions in shared memory and uses a lock file to serialize access to the sessions.

SSLSessionLockFile

`SSLSessionLockFile filename`

Contexts: GV   *Compatibility:* Stronghold
Default: `logs/session.lock`

Specifies the location of the session cache lock file.

The IBM HTTP server

On Unix platforms, the IBM HTTP Server uses a separate cache daemon program. Under Windows NT, the daemon is not used. The following directives are specific to this server.

SSLCachePath

`SSLCachePath filename`

Contexts: G   *Compatibility:* IHS

Specifies the pathname of the session ID cache daemon.

SSLCachePortFilename

SSLCachePortFilename *filename*

Contexts: G   *Compatibility:* IHS

Specifies the filename of the Unix domain socket used for communication between the child server processes and the cache daemon.

SSLCacheEnable

SSLCacheEnable

Contexts: G   *Compatibility:* IHS

Enables the cache daemon.

SSLCacheDisable

SSLCacheDisable

Contexts: G   *Compatibility:* IHS

Disables the cache daemon.

SSLCacheErrorLog

SSLCacheErrorLog *filename*

Contexts: G   *Compatibility:* IHS

Specifies the filename of the session cache error log.

SSLCacheTraceLog

SSLCacheTraceLog *filename*

Contexts: G   *Compatibility:* IHS

Specifies the filename of the log file for session ID trace messages.

Access Control Based on Protocol

SSLRequireSSL

SSLRequireSSL

Contexts: SF (AuthConfig)   *Compatibility:* mod_ssl 2.0, Apache-SSL

Forbids non-SSL access. Note that *mod_ssl* allows this directive only in a directory section or per-directory configuration file, while Apache-SSL allows the directive anywhere and uses the override FileInfo.

RequireSSL

RequireSSL

Contexts: GVSF (AuthConfig)   *Compatibility:* Stronghold

Forbids non-SSL access.

SSLDenySSL

SSLDenySSL

Contexts: GVSF (FileInfo)   *Compatibility:* Apache-SSL 1.36

Denies HTTPS connection attempts. HTTP connections are allowed.

SSLVersion

SSLVersion { SSLV2|SSLV3|ALL }

Contexts: GV   *Compatibility:* IHS

Rejects connections if the protocol version does not match the specified version.

SSLProtocol

SSLProtocol [+|-]*option*...

Contexts: GV   *Compatibility:* mod_ssl 2.2, Stronghold

Controls which protocol versions are allowed: SSLv2, SSLv3, and TLSv1. The keyword ALL stands for all protocols. Individual protocol version keywords may be prefixed with a plus sign (+) or minus sign (-) to add or remove that protocol from the list of protocols currently permitted.

Certificate-Based Access Controls

SSLVerifyClient

SSLVerifyClient *level*

Contexts: GV   *Compatibility:* mod_ssl 2.0, Apache-SSL, Stronghold

Specifies the level of certificate verification to be performed. Note that *mod_ssl* uses symbolic names, while Apache-SSL and Stronghold use numeric levels. Values for *level* are listed in the following table.

Value	Description
none (0)	No client certificate required.
optional (1)	Client may present a valid certificate.
require (2)	Client must present a valid certificate.

SSLClientAuth

SSLClientAuth { none|optional|required }

Contexts: GV   *Compatibility:* IHS

Specifies the level of certificate verification to be performed.

SSLVerifyDepth

SSLVerifyDepth *number*

Contexts: GV   *Compatibility:* mod_ssl 2.0, Apache-SSL, Stronghold
Default: 0

Specifies the number of CA certificates in the chain of certificates to be followed until a CA certificate is found that is held in the CA certificate path or file. A value of 0 means that only self-signed certificates are acceptable, while a value of 1 means that certificates must be signed by a CA that is directly known to the server.

Use of Cipher Suites

SSL uses public key cryptography only while establishing a session; symmetric encryption is used thereafter, as it is much faster. Cipher suites define the cryptographic algorithms used. These vary in strength and are listed in the following table.

Tag	Description
Key Exchange Algorithms	
kRSA	RSA key exchange
kDHr	Diffie-Hellman key exchange with RSA key
kDHu	Diffie-Hellman key exchange with DSA key
kEDH	Ephemeral Diffie-Hellman key exchange (no certificate)
Authentication Algorithms	
aNULL	No authentication
aRSA	RSA authentication
aDSS	DSS authentication
aDH	Diffie-Hellman authentication
Cipher Encoding Algorithms	
eNULL	No encoding
DES	DES encoding
3DES	Triple-DES encoding
RC4	RC4 encoding
RC2	RC2 encoding
IDEA	IDEA encoding
MAC Digest Algorithms	
MD5	MD5 hash function
SHA1	SHA1 hash function
SHA	SHA hash function
Aliases	
SSLv2	All SSL version 2.0 ciphers
SSLv3	All SSL version 3.0 ciphers

Tag	Description
EXP	All export-crippled ciphers
LOW	All low strength ciphers (no export, single DES)
MEDIUM	All ciphers with 128–bit encryption
HIGH	All ciphers that use Triple-DES
RSA	All ciphers that use RSA key exchange
DH	All ciphers that use Diffie-Hellman key exchange
EDH	All ciphers that use Ephemeral Diffie-Hellman key exchange
ADH	All ciphers that use Anonymous Diffie-Hellman key exchange
DSS	All ciphers that use DSS authentication
NULL	All ciphers that use no encryption

The IBM HTTP Server uses a different scheme for naming ciphers, as indicated by the following table. Note that cipher codes starting with the digit 2 are SSL version 2 ciphers, while those starting with 3 are SSL version 3 ciphers.

Code	Symbolic Name
27	SSL_DES_192_EDE3_CBC_WITH_MD5
21	SSL_RC4_128_WITH_MD5
23	SSL_RC2_CBC_128_CBC_WITH_MD5
26	SSL_DES_64_CBC_WITH_MD5
22	SSL_RC4_128_EXPORT40_WITH_MD5
24	SSL_RC2_CBC_128_CBC_EXPORT40_WITH_MD5
3A	SSL_RSA_WITH_3DES_EDE_CBC_SHA
35	SSL_RSA_WITH_RC4_128_SHA
34	SSL_RSA_WITH_RC4_128_MD5
39	SSL_RSA_WITH_DES_CBC_SHA
33	SSL_RSA_EXPORT_WITH_RC4_40_MD5
36	SSL_RSA_EXPORT_WITH_RC2_CBC_40_MD5
32	SSL_RSA_WITH_NULL_SHA

Code	Symbolic Name
31	SSL_RSA_WITH_NULL_MD5
30	SSL_NULL_WITH_NULL_NULL

The following directives control access bases on cipher suites.

SSLCipherSuite

`SSLCipherSuite cipher[:cipher]...`

Contexts: GVSF (AuthConfig)　　　　　　*Compatibility:* mod_ssl 2.1

Specifies a colon-separated string of cipher specifications defining the cipher suite the client is permitted to negotiate during the SSL handshake. In a per directory context, it forces an SSL renegotiation.

SSLRequiredCiphers

`SSLRequiredCiphers cipher[:cipher]...`

Contexts: GV　　　　　　　　　　　*Compatibility:* Apache-SSL

Specifies a colon-separated string of cipher specifications defining the cipher suite the client is permitted to negotiate during the SSL handshake.

SSLCipherList

`SSLCipherList cipher[:cipher]...`

Contexts: GV　　　　　　　　　　　*Compatibility:* Stronghold

Specifies a colon-separated string of cipher specifications defining the cipher suite the client is permitted to negotiate during the SSL handshake.

SSLCipherSpec

`SSLCipherSpec cipher...`

Contexts: GV*　　　　　　　　　　　*Compatibility:* IHS

Specifies a cipher that can be negotiated during the SSL handshake.

SSLProxyCipherList

`SSLProxyCipherList cipher[:cipher]...`

Contexts: GV   *Compatibility:* Stronghold

Specifies a colon-separated string of cipher specifications for server-side proxy connections.

SSLRequireCipher

`SSLRequireCipher cipher`

Contexts: GVSF* (FileInfo)   *Compatibility:* Apache-SSL, Stronghold

Specifies cipher types that are required in the current scope. Note that while Apache-SSL accepts a space-separated list of ciphers, Stronghold accepts only a single cipher.

SSLCipherRequire

`SSLCipherRequire cipher`

Contexts: GVSF* (FileInfo)   *Compatibility:* IHS

Specifies a cipher type that is required in the current scope.

SSLBanCipher

`SSLBanCipher cipher`

Contexts: GVSF* (FileInfo)   *Compatibility:* Apache-SSL, Stronghold

Specifies cipher types that are forbidden in the current scope. Note that while Apache-SSL accepts a space-separated list of ciphers, Stronghold accepts only a single cipher.

SSLCipherBan

`SSLCipherBan cipher`

Contexts: GVSF* (FileInfo)   *Compatibility:* IHS

Specifies a cipher type that is forbidden in the current scope.

Generalized Access Control Directives

mod_ssl, Stronghold, and the IBM HTTP Server provide generalized access control directives that allow arbitrary conditions to be specified, based on attributes of the components of the client certificate, or in the case of *mod_ssl*, based on any CGI or SSL variable. The syntax of the expressions varies among the four directives (SSLRequire, SSL_Require, SSL_Group, and SSLClientAuthRequire). Space precludes describing each syntax; refer to the appropriate server documentation for details.

Logging

SSL requests are logged to the configured transfer log, as for normal HTTP requests. However, Apache-SSL and *mod_ssl* add a %{*var*}x specifier to add the value of the named CGI/SSI variable to the log format. There is also a %{function}c specifier to log an SSL function.

Function	Description
version	SSL protocol version
cipher	SSL cipher
subjectdn	Client certificate subject DN
issuerdn	Client certificate issuer DN
errcode	Certificate verification numeric error code
errstr	Certificate verification error string

The following additional logging directives are mainly for debugging, as error conditions will normally be logged to Apache's error log file.

SSLLog

SSLLog *filename*

Contexts: GV   *Compatibility:* mod_ssl

Specifies the log file for the SSL engine. If the filename begins with a vertical bar (|) it is taken as the path of an executable program.

Relative filenames are assumed to be relative to the server root. Error messages are duplicated in the server error log.

SSLLogLevel

SSLLogLevel *level*

Contexts: GV   *Compatibility:* mod_ssl
Default: none

Specifies the amount of verbosity for logging to the SSL log file. *level* may be one of the keywords none, error, warn, info, trace or debug. Error messages are always written to the Apache error log file even if level is set to none.

SSLLogFile

SSLLogFile *filename*

Contexts: GV   *Compatibility:* Apache-SSL, Stronghold

Specifies the log file for the SSL engine.

SSLErrorFile

SSLErrorFile *filename*

Contexts: GV   *Compatibility:* Stronghold

Specifies the log file for errors occurring during SSL transactions.

SSL_CertificateLogDir

SSL_CertificateLogDir *directory*

Contexts: GV   *Compatibility:* Stronghold

Specifies the directory where client certificates are logged.

CGI Environment Variables

Standard CGI Variables

Variables not defined by the CGI specification are marked with a diamond (♦); HTTP request header field values are added to the environment with the prefix HTTP_; any hyphens in the header field name are changed to underscores.

AUTH_TYPE
: Authentication method (only if subject to authentication)

CONTENT_LENGTH
: Length of entity body (for POST requests, etc.)

CONTENT_TYPE
: MIME type of entity body (for POST requests, etc.)

DOCUMENT_ROOT♦
: Value of the DocumentRoot directive

GATEWAY_INTERFACE
: CGI version

PATH_INFO
: URL part after script identifier

PATH_TRANSLATED
: PATH_INFO translated into filesystem

QUERY_STRING
: Query string from URL (if present)

REMOTE_ADDR
: IP address of client

REMOTE_HOST
: DNS name of client (if resolved)

REMOTE_IDENT
: Remote user ID (unreliable, even if available)

REMOTE_USER
: Name of the authenticated user (only if the request is subject to authentication)

REQUEST_METHOD
: HTTP request method

SCRIPT_NAME
: Virtual path of the script

SERVER_ADMIN◆
    Value of the ServerAdmin directive

SERVER_ADDR
    IP address of the server

SERVER_NAME
    Hostname of the server

SERVER_PORT
    Port number of the server

SERVER_PROTOCOL
    Name and version of the protocol

SERVER_SOFTWARE
    Server software name and version

UNIQUE_ID◆
    Token that is unique across all requests (only if
    mod_unique_id is active)

Server-Side Include Variables

DATE_GMT
    Current date and time, expressed in GMT

DATE_LOCAL
    Current date and time, expressed in the local time zone

DOCUMENT_NAME
    Filename of the requested document, without any leading
    directory components

DOCUMENT_URI
    The %-decoded URL path of the requested document

LAST_MODIFIED
    The last modification time for the requested document

Additional mod_rewrite Variables

TIME
> Current date and time

TIME_YEAR
> Current year

TIME_MON
> Current month

TIME_DAY
> Current day of the month

TIME_HOUR
> Hour of the current day

TIME_MIN
> Minutes of the current hour

TIME_SEC
> Seconds of the current minute

TIME_WDAY
> Current day of the week

Additional SSL Variables

All secure versions of Apache add additional variables to the CGI/SSI environment. The following sections list these variables, noting in parentheses the versions of Apache that support each variable. Note that a diamond (♦) alongside *mod_ssl* indicates that the variable is only supported if the CompatEnvVars option is enabled.

The following table gives the names and descriptions of the components of the Distinguished Name (DN) of the subject and issuer of a certificate as used in SSL variables.

Component	Description
CN	Common name
O	Organization
OU	Organizational unit
L	Locality
ST	State or province (used by *mod_ssl*, IHS)
SP	State or province (used by Apache-SSL, Stronghold)
C	Country
EMAIL	Contact email address

SSL/TLS protocol information

HTTPS
Set if HTTPS is being used
(*mod_ssl*, Apache-SSL, IHS, Stronghold)

SSL_PROTOCOL
SSL protocol version (*mod_ssl*)

SSL_PROTOCOL_VERSION
SSL protocol version
(*mod_ssl*♦, Apache-SSL, IHS, Stronghold)

SSL_SESSION_ID
Hexadecimal-encoded SSL session ID (*mod_ssl*)

SSL_CIPHER
SSL/TLS cipherspec
(*mod_ssl*, Apache-SSL, IHS, Stronghold)

HTTPS_CIPHER
SSL/TLS cipherspec
(*mod_ssl*♦, Apache-SSL, IHS, Stronghold)

SSLEAY_VERSION
Version of SSLeay library
(*mod_ssl*♦, Apache-SSL, Stronghold)

SSL_VERSION_LIBRARY
> Version of OpenSSL library (*mod_ssl*)

SSL_VERSION_INTERFACE
> Version of *mod_ssl* (*mod_ssl*)

SSL_STRONG_CRYPTO
> Set to true if client is using strong cryptography, otherwise set to false (Stronghold)

HTTPS_KEYSIZE
> Size of the session key (IHS, Stronghold)

HTTPS_SECRETKEYSIZE
> Size of the secret key (IHS, Stronghold)

HTTPS_EXPORT
> Set if the session uses an export-grade (i.e., weak) cipher (Stronghold)

SSL_SERVER_SESSIONDIR
> Session caching directory (Stronghold)

SSL_SERVER_CERTIFICATELOGDIR
> Directory where client certificates are logged (Stronghold)

Server certificate information

SSL_SERVER_CERT
> PEM-encoded certificate (*mod_ssl* if the ExportCertData option is set)

SSL_SERVER_M_VERSION
> Certificate version (*mod_ssl*)

SSL_SERVER_M_SERIAL
> Certificate serial number (*mod_ssl*)

SSL_SERVER_A_SIG
> Algorithm used for signature of certificate (*mod_ssl*)

SSL_SERVER_SIGNATURE_ALGORITHM
> Algorithm used for signature of certificate (*mod_ssl*♦, Stronghold)

SSL_SERVER_A_KEY
    Algorithm used for public key of certificate (*mod_ssl*)

SSL_SERVER_V_START
    Start time of certificate validity (*mod_ssl*)

SSL_SERVER_CERT_START
    Start time of certificate validity (*mod_ssl*♦, Stronghold)

SSL_SERVER_V_END
    End time of certificate validity (*mod_ssl*)

SSL_SERVER_CERT_END
    End time of certificate validity (*mod_ssl*♦, Stronghold)

SSL_SERVER_S_DN
    Subject DN (*mod_ssl*)

SSL_SERVER_DN
    Subject DN (*mod_ssl*♦, Apache-SSL, IHS, Stronghold)

SSL_SERVER_S_*component*
    Component of server's DN (*mod_ssl*)

SSL_SERVER_*component*
    Component of server's DN
    (*mod_ssl*♦, Apache-SSL, IHS, Stronghold)

SSL_SERVER_I_DN
    Issuer DN (*mod_ssl*)

SSL_SERVER_IDN
    Issuer DN (*mod_ssl*♦, Apache-SSL, IHS, Stronghold)

SSL_SERVER_I_*component*
    Component of issuer DN (*mod_ssl*)

SSL_SERVER_I*component*
    Component of issuer DN
    (*mod_ssl*♦, Apache-SSL, IHS, Stronghold)

Client certificate information

Client certificate environment variables are set only if client authentication is enabled.

SSL_CLIENT_CERT
> PEM-encoded certificate (*mod_ssl* if the ExportCertData option is set)

SSL_CLIENT_CERT_CHAIN*n*
> PEM-encoded certificate *n* in certificate chain (Apache-SSL if the SSLExportClientCertificates directive is specified)

SSL_CLIENT_M_VERSION
> Certificate version (*mod_ssl*)

SSL_CLIENT_M_SERIAL
> Certificate serial number (*mod_ssl*)

SSL_CLIENT_SERIALNUM
> Certificate serial number (IHS)

SSL_CLIENT_A_SIG
> Algorithm used for signature of certificate (*mod_ssl*)

SSL_CLIENT_SIGNATURE_ALGORITHM
> Algorithm used for signature of certificate (*mod_ssl*♦, Stronghold)

SSL_CLIENT_A_KEY
> Algorithm used for public key of certificate (*mod_ssl*)

SSL_CLIENT_V_START
> Start time of certificate validity (*mod_ssl*)

SSL_CLIENT_CERT_START
> Start time of certificate validity (*mod_ssl*♦, Stronghold)

SSL_CLIENT_V_END
> End time of certificate validity (*mod_ssl*)

SSL_CLIENT_CERT_END
> End time of certificate validity (*mod_ssl*♦, Stronghold)

`SSL_CLIENT_VERIFY`
Validity of certificate (*mod_ssl*)

`SSL_CLIENT_S_DN`
Subject DN (*mod_ssl*)

`SSL_CLIENT_DN`
Subject DN (*mod_ssl*♦, Apache-SSL, IHS, Stronghold)

`SSL_CLIENT_S_component`
Component of subject DN (*mod_ssl*)

`SSL_CLIENT_component`
Component of subject DN
(*mod_ssl*♦, Apache-SSL, IHS, Stronghold)

`SSL_CLIENT_I_DN`
Issuer DN (*mod_ssl*)

`SSL_CLIENT_IDN`
Issuer DN (*mod_ssl*♦, Apache-SSL, IHS)

`SSL_CLIENT_I_component`
Component of issuer DN (*mod_ssl*)

`SSL_CLIENT_Icomponent`
Component of issuer DN (*mod_ssl*♦, Apache-SSL, IHS)

`SSL_CLIENT_CERT_BODY`
Client certificate as a string (IHS)

`SSL_CLIENT_CERT_BODY_LEN`
Length of the client certificate string (IHS)

`SSL_CLIENT_SESSSIONID`
Session ID (IHS)

`SSL_CLIENT_NEW_SESSSIONID`
Set to "TRUE" if the session ID is new (IHS)

`SSL_CLIENT_SERIALNUM`
Client certificate serial number (IHS)

Index of Apache Directives

More Titles from O'Reilly

Web Programming

Java Servlet Programming

By Jason Hunter with William Crawford
1st Edition November 1998
528 pages, ISBN 1-56592-391-X

Dynamic HTML:
The Definitive Reference

By Danny Goodman
1st Edition July 1998
1088 pages, ISBN 1-56592-494-0

Frontier: The Definitive Guide

By Matt Neuburg
1st Edition February 1998
616 pages, ISBN 1-56592-383-9

JavaScript: The Definitive Guide,
3rd Edition

By David Flanagan
3rd Edition June 1998
800 pages, ISBN 1-56592-392-8

Learning VBScript

By Paul Lomax
1st Edition July 1997
616 pages, Includes CD-ROM
ISBN 1-56592-247-6

ASP in a Nutshell

By A. Keyton Weissinger
1st Edition February 1999
426 pages, ISBN 1-56592-490-8

Writing Apache Modules
with Perl and C

By Lincoln Stein & Doug MacEachern
1st Edition March 1999
746 pages, ISBN 1-56592-567-X

Webmaster in a Nutshell,
2nd Edition

By Stephen Spainbour & Robert Eckstein
2nd Edition June 1999
540 pages, ISBN 1-56592-325-1

DocBook: The Definitive Guide

By Norman Walsh & Leonard Muellner
1st Edition October 1999
652 pages, Includes CD-ROM
ISBN 1-56592-580-7

JavaScript Application Cookbook

By Jerry Bradenbaugh
1st Edition September 1999
478 pages, ISBN 1-56592-577-7

Practical Internet Groupware

By Jon Udell
1st Edition October 1999
524 pages, ISBN 1-56592-537-8

O'REILLY®

TO ORDER: *800-998-9938* • *order@oreilly.com* • *http://www.oreilly.com/*
OUR PRODUCTS ARE AVAILABLE AT A BOOKSTORE OR SOFTWARE STORE NEAR YOU.
FOR INFORMATION: *800-998-9938* • *707-829-0515* • *info@oreilly.com*